How To Make Big Money Trading In All Financial Conditions

Simon Watkins

ADVFN BOOKS

This book is dedicated to my son, James Harper-Watkins

CONTENTS

Changing Volatility Patterns

Only God moves in mysterious ways: pretty much everything else works to patterns. Despite what some people might say even in periods of low market volatility (the measure of deviation of market prices from the average mean price over a specified period of time, of course), **there is always some asset, somewhere in the world, that is oscillating in price sufficiently that you can trade it to make serious money every day of the week that a market is open.**

The trick is to know what the asset is, whether it is trading generally higher or lower than it should be on a fundamental and technical basis (and for what reasons) and to have the skill, speed of thought and tenacity to stick it out, through hedges where appropriate, when everybody else thinks that you are wrong.

In broad terms, the first thing to be aware of is that **ever since the onset of the global financial crisis in 2007/2008, broad market volatility has settled at much lower average levels than was the case before the crisis.**

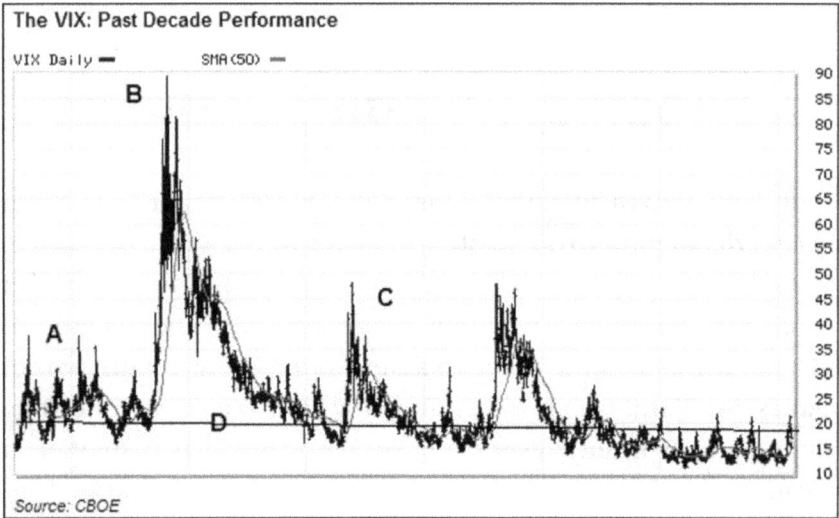

The VIX: Past Decade Performance

Source: CBOE

[Chart Key:
A= Asian Crisis
B = Global Financial Crisis
C = Eurozone periphery sovereign crisis
D = Average volatility]

The Changed Role Of
Central Banks Since The Crisis

The reason for this – and this is still a key factor of which to be aware, as it forms the backdrop to the current trading environment – is the changing role of the world's major central banks since the world's financial system nearly collapsed.

Prior to the financial crisis, the world's central banks' principal, and often sole, responsibility with regard to their currencies, was overall price stability. Since then their remits have broadened out to include a range of socio-economic

targets, such as employment levels, interest rates, inflation and so forth.

As a corollary of these new concerns, **many central banks, particularly those of the G10, have been engaged in 'smoothing operations' of FX volatility since the crisis, sometimes working in tandem.**

In practical terms, if you are the Bank of England and you are looking to create a broad economic climate that is conducive to increasing employment levels, for example, then you do not want sterling to keep appreciating beyond a certain level as, if it does, British goods and services become far more expensive abroad relative to those of Britain's competitors, exports decline and businesses lay off workers.

This explains why **the global Volatility Index – 'VIX' – found on the Chicago Board Options Exchange (CBOE) website, under the symbol 'VIX' (specifically: http://www.cboe.com/micro/VIX/vixintro.aspx) has spent most of the recent past trading at, or near to, historically low levels.**

However, it is equally important to realise that even in times when overall market volatility may be extremely historically low, this **does not reflect a multitude of much higher intra-regional volatility offering pockets of value in different asset classes around the globe (we are coming onto these).**

The VIX itself, for example, only measures the implied volatility of the options bought and sold on the S&P500 US stock index, which is generally regarded as being the asset most susceptible to changes in risk appetite by investors.

It is even more important for the retail trader, though, to understand what the individual global central banks are hoping to achieve in broad terms and how this translates into their currencies, because **although a currency might not be moving up and down a lot it might still be headed in one direction overall, allowing** for a pure 'value' or 'momentum' (directional) trade that can make a lot of relatively risk-free money.

Fundamentals Really Matter
In Low Volatility Markets

In fact, for the intelligent retail trader, **low volatility markets can be regarded as a gift from the market gods,** provided that they work out exactly what a particular central bank is looking to achieve from its currency and then monitor fundamental developments along the way.

In the following sub-section, we are going to take a quick look at how the individual fundamental factors have dictated the course of the 'Big Four' central banks and their currencies (and continue to do so), as indicated by their daily trading volumes and their exclusive inclusion in the IMF's Special Drawing Rights (SDRs): the BOJ (JPY), the ECB (EUR), the Fed (USD) and the Bank of England (GBP).

The Bank of Japan (BOJ)

The BOJ and, as a corollary, the yen (JPY) have been great examples of the above approach over the past couple of years or so and should continue to provide alpha returns in the coming years as well, based almost entirely on fundamentals.

When Shinzo Abe became Prime Minister of Japan at the end of 2012, he faced a situation in which the country had been stuck in a decade-long period of economic stagnation, made worse by a strong JPY that made exports more expensive relative to competitor nations (especially its newly-invigorated regional ones, including places like Thailand, South Korea, Malaysia and even more recently Vietnam and Cambodia). The JPY was under even more pressure to appreciate from foreign investors, especially hedge funds.

USDJPY (3 Years, Daily)

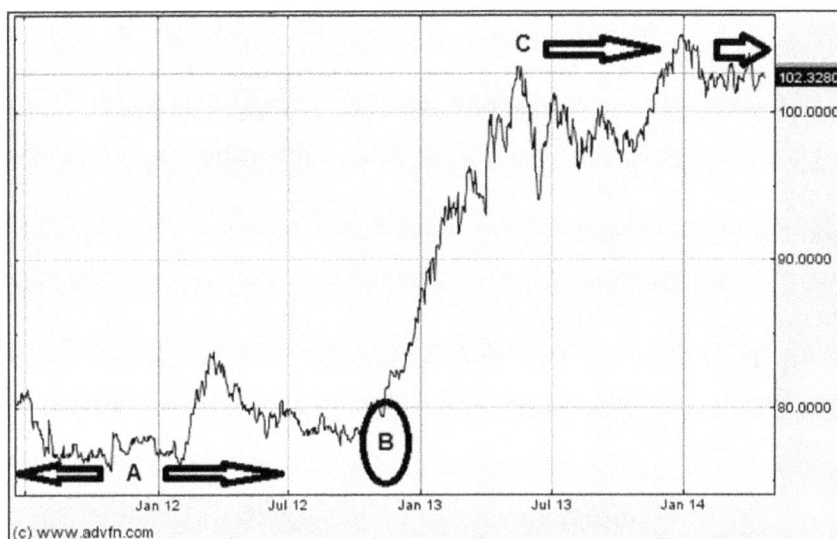

[Chart Key:

A = USDJPY around the 75.00 level, already making Japan's exports uncompetitive, prompting the BOJ to step in repeatedly to buy USD and sell JPY under heavy JPY buying by hedge funds in particular

B = Shinzo Abe becomes PM in December 2012, announcing a new economy-expanding agenda

C = USDJPY appreciation stalls, as markets question the economic follow-through for Abe's plans]

As can be seen from the chart above, the Bank of Japan had been buying USD and selling JPY very aggressively in order to support its export market (and thus to ensure that the economy did not stagnate even further) from around the USDJPY75.00 level, whilst many major market players – especially hedge funds – were selling USD and buying JPY anywhere above 80.00.

Multi-Pronged Central Bank Intervention

It was only when, in fact, the Bank of Japan was tasked with ensuring a broad-based policy strategy – engineering sustained nominal annual economic growth of 3% (there had been no average annual nominal GDP growth for 15 years) and at least a 2% annual inflation rate every year from 2015, as well as commencing a massive domestic bond-buying QE programme (Fed-style) – that the JPY managed sustained depreciation of the sort wanted by Abe and moved through the key USDJPY100 resistance level and beyond.

In this instance, the smart retail trader would have noticed two things, in order, at the end of December 2012/beginning of January 2013:

1. That **the entire policy remit of the BOJ had altered to a sea-change of the 'once in a lifetime' variety** and that this, by logical extension, would mean that the yen had to weaken for the policy directives to be met

2. That **key resistance levels were being broken on a weekly basis,** as shown below.

USDJPY (3 Years, Daily)

[Chart Key:
A to G = Previous resistance levels, all broken, very quickly
ABE PM = Shinzo Abe takes over as Prime Minister]

Once Abe was more firmly ensconced as PM, this battle between those who sought to protect their shorts moved up the values on USDJPY, as the BOJ employed even more QE and greater scope on Forward Guidance as a means of manipulating the JPY to make it weaker. Underlining my point about volatility, readers will note that price swings have been very few and far between, even intra-day, but rather have moved firmly one way (upwards) until USDJPY stalled.

In practical terms this means that it was a gift from the dealing gods.

If, for example, you had noticed the two points I outlined above, **just on a straight GBP10 per pip even after three or four resistance levels had broken, without even adding to longs and averaging up, the returns would have been GBP17,000.**

This trade would have been initiated after four breaks of previous resistance levels, at 85.50 (a major multiple resistance point) with a stop loss order at 84.50 (major support), meaning a possible total loss of GBP1000 but with a target of 94.50 (another major resistance level), meaning a total potential upside of GBP9000.

USDJPY (3 Years, Daily)

[Chart Key:
A = Buy USDJPY @ 85.50, GBP10 per point
S = Stop loss sell @ 84.50
T = Target initially of 94.50]

The risk/reward ratio would have been 9:1 in your favour. As I highlighted in my previous book, *'Everything You Need To Know About Making Serious Money Trading The Financial Markets'*, and as I will reiterate later in this book, **it is extremely unwise for any new, or even experienced, trader to enter into a trade in which they do not stand to gain at least four times the amount that they could**

lose from a trade, given key support and resistance levels (*see later section on Risk Management on page 112*).

The European Central Bank (ECB)

The European Union – and, by extension, the ECB and the euro (EUR) – has always been a massive disaster waiting to happen, albeit we have seen some mini-disasters along the way from the euro's creation in 1999 (the ruination of Greece, Spain, Portugal and Ireland, together with a number of still pending possible calamities, including most notably Italy and France).

The basic problem underlying the Union remains and is best to be borne in mind for future reference when contemplating taking out long-term longs in it, that the inhabitants of Europe do not broadly think of themselves in notional ideological terms as being 'European' or even Northern European or Southern European, but rather in practical nationalistic terms as being German, French, Italian and so on.

Fundamental Ideological Disconnects

In this profoundly basic context, a paradox lies at the heart of the European Union: it is designed to create a pan-European identity amongst a diverse range of peoples who fundamentally do not, and never have, seen themselves as anything other than citizens of nation states, each with their own individual language, culture, history and traditions.

This is why the once much-vaunted pan-European language of Esperanto still has but a handful of speakers and is not the language of business in the region. It is also why there is neither a common EU foreign policy, nor one of defence, nor indeed – and this is at the epicentre of previous crises – shared fiscal or wider budgetary policies.

Further still, this fundamental nationalism across EU states means that there is an endemic reluctance on the part of the more industrialised and wealthier countries of Northern Europe to assist the softer economies of Southern Europe, particularly when they are regarded as profligate.

The euro compounds all of these problems, especially when, as in recent times, it has been strong, as it means that **the ECB always has to conduct a high-wire balancing act of stunning delicacy to:**

1. **Make sure that the EUR does not appreciate way beyond the level that entirely chokes off export-driven growth** across the region (although it has come remarkably close to doing this in the past); and,

2. **Ensure that markets do not get spooked by bearish talk** and sell the hell out of the currency, prompting another aggressive and local economy-ruining assault on the domestic bond markets of its constituent members.

We will come onto the reason why it occasionally goes into bullish mode in a moment, as spotting when this trend is subject to reversal is a key for trading it.

The Importance Of Global FX Reserve Management Strategy

I would posit that the reason for the euro's enduring incremental strength over the levels where it should probably be trading is simply that as the US Federal Reserve Bank (Fed) printed an unprecedented amount of USD in its QE programme, **many FX reserve managers shifted towards a more active approach where investment and diversification become pivotal.** For a select few reserve managers tied to the USD – and thus Fed policy – via their passive receipts, this new strategy led to ongoing 'USD-recycling', or rebalancing, into a broader portfolio of currencies, most notably the EUR.

Indeed, **some market players estimated these 'hidden' EUR reserve holdings by central bank reserve managers at over USD3 trillion as at the end of the first quarter of 2014 alone** (when the EUR was still otherwise bewilderingly bid), and this process has continued to provide a significant source of artificial support for the currency against the run of fundamentals.

Nonetheless, the prospect of the ECB employing a Fed-type QE programme, or of injecting liquidity by other means, into the Eurozone's economy as a whole, needs to be watched out for.

Having said that, again employing a one-direction strategy would have worked perfectly, especially if taken in tandem with hedging positions for a possible fall out for the periphery EU states.

Business and Consumer Confidence Numbers

Two key data releases in particular at which traders should look for the euro is the business and consumer confidence numbers. Organisations/governments love to produce these indices (often on a scale of 0-100, where 100 is super-confident, 0 is as confident as one would be when an automated bank telephone system tells you that it is dealing with your inquiry and anywhere above 50 shows overall optimism) for both of the above-mentioned categories, so make sure that you know which ones to take seriously.

Aside from those pertaining directly to the eurozone itself, at least as important is the **German IFO** number – again a business confidence index – which shows how confident or not businesses are of future prospects on a scale of 0-100.

EURUSD (2 Years, Daily)

[Chart Key:
A = Long EUR @ 1.2779, GBP10 per pip, as multiple support levels hold and additional bullish support confirmation coming from 38.2% Fibonacci level holding
B = Sell as head and shoulders look threatened at 1.3890
Total Profit = GBP11,110]

The Importance Of Looking At Different Timescales Of Charts

This, by the way, raises an interesting point about **the timescales of charts that you look at**. The above chart shows a clear bull trend on EURUSD, leading one to think, perhaps – if you are of a bullish EUR bent – that it has probably topped out at around the 1.3900 level.

Look again, this time at a longer-dated chart:

EURUSD (6 Years, Weekly)

(c) www.advfn.com

[Chart Key:
A = Top and beginning of overall downtrend
B = Downtrend endures, compounded by debt crises in EU periphery sovereign
states
C = Relative short-term bull move]

The point is this: **it is highly advisable to look back as far as the
charts will allow in order to glean the whole picture.** In the above
example, a long, short-term, looks perfectly justified but it should be
taken out in the knowledge that a major reversal could occur at any
point, given certain catalysts.

The Federal Reserve Bank (Fed)

For a very long time, there had been a much-vaunted notion that the
US dollar was on the verge of a new long-term trading uptrend (*see
chart below*).

The realisation of this, though, remained stymied by the type of broader policy mandate for the Fed that I mentioned earlier. In particular, this was that the central bank's massive bond buying QE programme – and any rises to interest rates as a corollary – would remain in place at least until the US's unemployment rate settled at or below the 6.5% level.

What The FOMC Says Is At Least As Important As What It Actually Does

Again, though, **the importance of staying up to date with such apparently mundane items as the minutes from central bank meetings and ad hoc statements from key central bankers was proven** as the notion of a long-term upwards re-rating of the USD came back into play after Fed Chair, Janet Yellen, in March 2014 implied that the Bank's long-held 6.5% jobless threshold for even considering hiking interest rates was to be discarded.

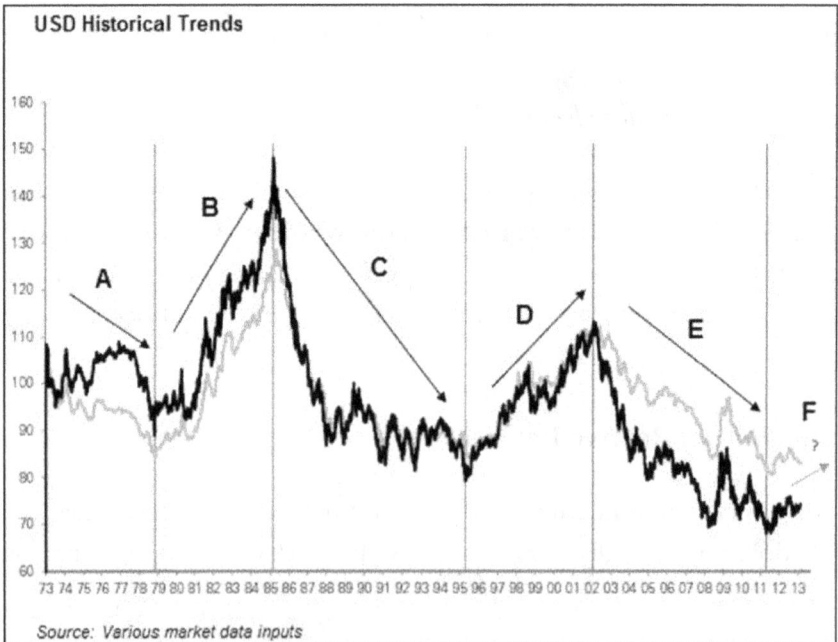

USD Historical Trends

Source: Various market data inputs

[Chart Key:
Lines
Upper dark black from left to right = Nominal US dollar versus majors
Lower light black from left to right = Real broad US dollar
Vertical lines = Key trend turning points
Arrows From Left To Right
A = 6 years, down 18%
B = 6 years, up 67%
C = 10 years, down 46%
D = 7 years, up 43%
E = 9 years, down 40%
F = Next big trend . . . UP?]

With US financial policy makers having linked stimulus to employment and inflation for the first time in December 2012 and the target for US overnight interest rates having been 0-0.25% since December 2008, the 'USD uptrend theory' had been stuck in an environment where risk sentiment was not sufficiently buoyed by US growth to see inflows into US assets, but not sufficiently gloomy about an EM slowdown to see safe haven inflows either.

But it was not just the abandonment of the jobless threshold that lifted the USD Index from its previous four month lows but also Yellen's accompanying comment that the timing of the first hike after the end of the QE bond buying programme could well be even earlier than anybody had expected.

In practical terms, whether this was what Yellen intended to say or not – as she repeatedly stated that FOMC policy had not changed – the markets took the comments to suggest a greater Fed willingness to tighten than had earlier been expressed and the USD could not have asked for anything better than the prospect of a stiffening of two years' yields.

FOMC Meetings With Accompanying Press Conferences Are Especially Important

FOMC meetings with press conferences have consistently generated large moves (volume, volatility and price) and much larger price changes than meetings without press conferences.

For example, as the chart below illustrates, in terms of volatility to begin with, USD/JPY moves are consistently large on FOMC press conference days when compared with days when the FOMC finishes with only the regular statement.

The smallest absolute percentage change in USD/JPY on an FOMC press conference day is 0.42%, which is the second largest absolute change on an FOMC day when only a statement is released! The same pattern is evident in EUR/USD where the median of the absolute percentage change in EUR/USD was 0.65% on press conference days and a very subdued 0.20% median on days when FOMC ended with no press conference. The above message was largely echoed in equities price action and slightly less so in Treasuries.

Median Of The Absolute 1 Day Change In Selected Asset Markets When The FOMC Does & Does Not Have A Press Conference						
	S&P 500 (% change)	2 yr yield (change in bps)	10 yr yield (change in bps)	USD/EUR (% change)	USD/JPY (% change)	USD/AUD (% change)
Press conference	0.94	2	6	0.65	0.91	0.54
No press conference	0.35	1	4	0.20	0.34	0.50
Source: EcoWin, Federal Reserve Board						

As an adjunct to this, there is a strong bias for FOMC press conference days to result in higher 10yr yields (6 of last 8 meetings) and a very similar story of USD/JPY going up. By contrast, the USD generally over the course of the first half of 2014 and the latter half of 2013 had a downward bias versus the EUR on press conference days, but showed no directional bias on non-press conference FOMC days.

Interest Rates Are Paramount

Indeed, **interest rates are perhaps the key determinant in FX rates globally**. Remember, money goes to where it is best rewarded. All other factors remaining equal, if one country raises its interest rates to above those of another country then the former's currency will become stronger than the latter's as investment capital moves from the latter to the former.

Interest rates, in basic terms, are a key tool for a government in managing its economy. **If an economy is becoming overheated – i.e. inflation is increasing to beyond the point at which a government deems it healthy – then interest rates will go up. (A little inflation is a healthy thing, anything from 1% to 5% as a rule of thumb, depending on whether an economy is 'developed', 'emerging' or 'frontier': see later.)** This means in practical terms that money becomes more expensive, people spend less, demand decreases, manufacturers cannot increase their prices and thus prices stay the same. And, of course, the converse is true.

The last few years in the West are instructive in this context. In the UK, for example, interest rates were low for many years, meaning that people could borrow money (from banks, on credit cards and so on) for very little in terms of interest repayments. As such, prices increased, the stock market boomed, house prices boomed and people had lots of 'things' (largely things which they did not need, of course). Eventually this resulted in a housing and stock market bubble, which then spent years bursting.

In fact, this low interest rate scenario usually has the effect of increasing inflation – that is, more people are in a position to buy, for example, a DVD player, and thus the makers of DVD players raise their prices, increase supply or both. If inflation is not contained in this scenario then there is the danger that it will spiral out of control, meaning that eventually the increasing price of DVD players would reach such a level that people would have to ask for pay rises. More pay would mean more money in the economy, which would mean more DVD players being sold, which would mean prices going up further, which means more pay rises and so on and so forth: a never-ending upwards spiral, the logical conclusion of which was found in Weimar Germany where a wheelbarrow full of currency was eventually required to buy a loaf of bread. Or even today in countries such as Zimbabwe, in which the currency has become meaningless pieces of paper. Indeed, using our UK scenario, in the midst of such increasing supply of money, the value of GBP would collapse as a product of supply and demand. In this event, interest rates would have to rise to curtail price increases and the converse is true.

Inflation Rates Are A Key Driver Of Sentiment

Consequently, **when figures are released showing that inflation in a country looks to be headed upwards, towards levels that a government will not tolerate, dealers believe that the likelihood of interest rates being increased has been raised and thus the currency is likely to appreciate and the currency will be bought.** And, of course, the converse is true.

The chart below shows the effect that an anticipated increase in interest rates had on the NZD in June 2010; incidentally, this rise was due to growing inflationary pressures in the country. Speculation that the New Zealand government would raise rates began around 8 June; the actual rise was on 10 June.

NZDUSD (4 Years, Weekly)

FX:NZDUSD (New Zealand Dollar (B) VS United States Dollar Spot (Nzd/USD))
Open: 0.8376 High: 0.8432 Low: 0.835 Cur: 0.8394 (+00.00185/+00.22%)

[Chart Key:
A = Market hears rumours that bolster expectations that the central bank will
raise interest rates
B = Interest rates hikes are announced]

It is apposite to note here that **there are two key inflation figures released by most countries: the Consumer Price Index (CPI) and the Producers Price Index (PPI)**. The United Kingdom also introduced the Retail Price Index, which includes items such as housing, which the government tends to play down, as it is often much worse for political purposes than the CPI.

The former can be viewed as prices relating to what people have to spend on a day to day basis to keep their lives ticking over: food, travel, clothing and so on, and this is the more important of the two inflation measures. The latter, in the meantime, deals with expenses that producers of the things people buy incur: machinery, fuel, staplers and so on.

It is wise to note that rises/falls in the PPI are often a precursor to the same in the CPI. This makes sense from the cost-push inflationary aspect as if the prices of raw materials/services used to make goods go up (PPI) then the price of goods/services will tend to go up (CPI).

So, Yellen's comments were instructive for traders and they reacted according to future expectations of interest rates, without the encumbrance of any other factor, as seen below.

EURUSD (6 Months, Daily)

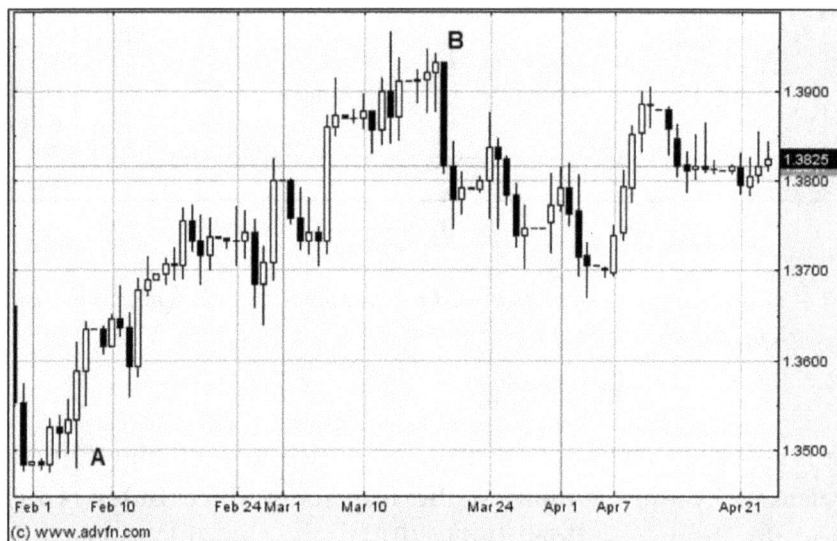

[Chart Key:
A = Markets still in the collective mindset that there will be no change to US interest rate policy for the foreseeable future
B = Yellen's statements about discarding the 6.5% unemployment factor in raising interest rates causing a sharp strengthening of the USD]

This again underlines the importance of fundamentals when dealing in low volatility markets. Yes, volatility remained below

the historical average, but a simple buy of USD and sale of EUR at the time of the Yellen comments would have netted 230 pips in just over a week.

It is apposite to note that although the straight cause and effect between the unemployment rate and the end of QE/onset of a rates hiking cycle appears no longer to exist, the US Non-Farm Payrolls figure is still a critical number to watch. This is released by the US Department of Labor Statistics at 8:30am US Eastern time on the first Friday of every month. It estimates the total number of paid workers in the US, excluding those working in: the Government, private household employees, non-profit organisations and farm workers. Together, 'non-farm' employees account for about 80% of US GDP.

Expectations Are Often More Important than Reality

As with all figures, major or minor, it is not so much a case of what the figure actually is or what it means for an economy but rather how it compares to market expectations of what it should be. Hence, if, as demonstrated below, the market believes that US employment is likely to increase at a certain level but the figure comes in at a level lower than those expectations then that country's currency will fall.

The chart below shows the effect of the anticipation that previous estimates that employment conditions would continue to improve significantly were mistaken.

USDCHF (1 Year, Daily)

FX:USDCHF (United States Dollar (B) VS Swiss Franc Spot (USD/Chf))
Open: 0.899 High: 0.9032 Low: 0.8984 Cur: 0.9011 (+00.00215/+00.24%)

[Chart Key:
A = release of numbers showing that the rate of recent declines in the US unemployment figures slowed, raising some questions about the sustainability of the US Federal Reserve's intention to continue to taper down its buying of bonds for quantitative easing purposes]

Two problems of which to be aware in trading NFP figures are: first, that they **tend to be revised at various points close to the initial announcement** (and thus, a **false move** is very common – e.g. a move down followed by a move up or vice-versa); and second, **they are released at a time when there are very few major market participants in the market** (London traders are generally down the pub by that time on a Friday, New York traders are probably making their way to their country houses in Connecticut and Asia is asleep), so these moves **tend to be very violent** one way and then the other.

The Bank Of England (BOE)

Sterling has been the beneficiary, or not (from the UK government's perspective), of the 'least ugly in the beauty contest' concept for some time, given ongoing QE from the US and Japan (plus Japan's other stated economy-boosting policies) and from jitters over deflationary pressures and credit worthiness of periphery sovereigns in the eurozone.

Going back to basics, two things were clear about the rally in GBP that rolled into the first part of 2014:

1. That against the other majors, GBP was, by default, the winning trade, and thus a short-term long was called for.

2. Longer-term, as the factors that made the other majors weak eroded, the focus would shift back onto the UK's own fundamentals, which, whilst not outright bad, actually bear little close scrutiny (e.g. growth was still largely consumer- and credit-led, rather than via a material increase in exports, or the domestic manufacturing base – a situation, in fact, exactly like that which prompted the credit crisis a few years back), demanding a longer-term short.

GBPUSD (1 Year, Daily)

[Chart Key:

A = Go long, having seen a break to the upside through previously strong resistance at 1.5180, GBP10 per pip

B = Add to long, GBP10 per pip, as another major triple resistance point is breached and technicals and fundamentals for the USD and the other majors look weak, at 1.6180

C = On triple resistance point and Yellen discarding the 6.5% consideration for US interest rate rises, liquidate all positions, at 1.6780

Total Profit = GBP22,000]

One way of getting to hard numbers on how far overvalued sterling looked in Q1 2014 was by comparing the levels with a 5-year moving average, which focused only on the most recent period.

This showed GBP to be about 5% 'overvalued', although the most extreme 'undervaluation' relative to the 5 year average was about 20%

in 2008 (but it had been 15-17% 'undervalued' on several occasions over the full period).

This again suggested that there was up to another 20% further for GBP to fall before it would pose no major problems for the currency or the UK, given that it was still around 5% overvalued.

This would mean GBPUSD at 1.2160, but a more realistic target would probably be nearer the 1.3500 level, all other things remaining equal.

Other Central Banks And Currency Wars

Up until global growth began to stutter, countries used to accept the notion that they might lose more of the available regional trade to a neighbour that was depreciating its currency because the world's overall economic pie was growing and their share net/net would still be growing as well.

In recent times, though, in a world of anaemic, if any, economic growth across the globe, currency depreciation by a neighbour makes this a **zero-sum game, in which one neighbour's currency depreciation means a neighbour empirically losing out on the available international trade and investment capital flows.**

With the stakes so raised, central banks have been inclined to use a much broader array of policies to ensure their country comes out on top, way over and above direct intervention in the FX markets that used to be the principal weapon of choice. These tactics are set to endure in ongoing 'currency wars', although, as growth does return globally, they will be more sporadic and geographically specific.

As the scale of the US's economic recovery remains uncertain, China's growth trajectory looks pressured from now on and major questions hang over the nature of economic growth in the eurozone and Japan, the key focus for many of the world's central banks in the coming months will be on inflation figures.

With inflation declining in many countries, fears of disinflation or of outright deflation are growing, and in that environment there is a general desire to avoid currency strength as it would only increase deflationary pressures.

Clearly, we all know by now that the two major currencies to have been at the receiving end of massive intervention – direct, rhetorical and interest rate related – are the Japanese yen and the Swiss franc, but to a lesser degree a great many currencies have dabbled to a greater or lesser degree in all/a couple/one of these intervention tactics particularly over the recent past.

In general geographical terms, there has been a notable hardening of attitudes in **Latin America**, with the CLP, COP and PEN all moved for some time towards greater intervention to counter fundamentals-driven appreciation of their currencies (in these cases, as a result of rising commodities prices). More specifically here, they all reduced interest rates, to little effect, and then embarked on other measures: Colombia (big in a range of commodities) scaled back its 2013 overseas borrowing plan to reduce its foreign debt and increased its daily USD purchases; Chile (the biggest copper exporter in the world) added to its USD selling markedly; and Peru (hugely rich in silver and other commodities) undertook a raft of new measures including announcing that it will pay back foreign debt earlier than expected.

Looking at the combinations of different actions and situations recently, for example, the yen looks relatively undervalued now but is still the most active in terms of depreciation efforts. By contrast, most of the valuation scores within **EMEA** are comparatively low and stable, with the notable exception of the Turkish lira (TRY), which is currently playing the same game as Japan.

For its part, the Swiss franc has been the recipient of attempts to reduce its value, but its safe-haven asset status has still meant that it attracts more flows than the SNB thinks is good for it.

Interestingly as well, the position of **Asian currencies ex-Japan** is less marked now than it was in 2012. Intervention in currency markets has long been a favoured tactic in this region, but the approach seems to have moved away from a one-sided limiting of appreciation towards a two-sided limiting of volatility instead ('smoothing operations'). In the meantime, the RUB and CNY are pushing more towards currency regime liberalisation, the TWD and KRW are seeking to lower the volatility rather than the value of their currencies and the BRL has also become less combative over the last year, a stance consistent with its less overvalued currency – a measure perhaps of the success of its earlier interventionist ways.

Many of these countries, by the way, are discussed in greater detail in Section Three of this book, *Finding Value in Emerging Markets* on page 65.

The Return Of The Enduring Carry Trade

From around 2003 to the onset of the global financial crisis in 2007/08 the carry trade (in which an investor sells a certain currency with a relatively low interest rate, like yen or Swiss franc (CHF) or Norwegian krone (NOK) and uses the funds to purchase a different currency yielding a higher interest rate) was the key driver for many in the FX market.

That was until the dramatically rising volatilities across the currency world made the funding side of the two part trade increasingly hazardous (clearly, there is no point in doing this type of trade if the interest rate gain is wiped out by an adverse currency movement).

At that point, 'risk on risk off' (RORO) strategies (*more of these in Section Two on page 42*) were the preferred weapon of choice for most dealers up to the middle of 2012 when developments at the US Fed, Europe's ECB and Japan's BOJ, in particular, served to re-focus traders' attention back on expectations for the monetary policies of the world's central banks.

Now, though, **with the Fed having begun to taper its quantitative easing programme whilst the BOJ remains on the course of a 2% inflation target and a 3% nominal GDP rate, and a growing view that the ECB may be about to embark on its own bond-buying programme, divergence in interest rates may herald the return of the carry trade as a dominant FX strategy.**

Whilst the direct benefits of such a strategy are minimal for the retail trader (some dealing platforms will give you a rebate on a short JPY, CHF or NOK position, or one for a similar funding currency, position) **the indirect benefits of tracking the return of the carry trade across all applicable currencies can be huge.**

For example, one of the key reasons why the JPY continued to weaken, despite growing misgivings in the markets about whether the BOJ's economic strategy would pan out, was its use on the funding side of the carry trade for many.

And the same can be said about pullbacks on the CHF, as seen below, just after the Fed's Yellen made her comments that pertained to the future timing and scope of interest rate rises in the US (thus increasing the interest rate differential between the US and Switzerland, in the US's favour).

Even though the USD itself had been used as a funding currency for some time – given its near zero interest rates – the mere prospect of an increased interest rate differential between the two caused a spike in USDCHF.

USDCHF (6 Months, Daily)

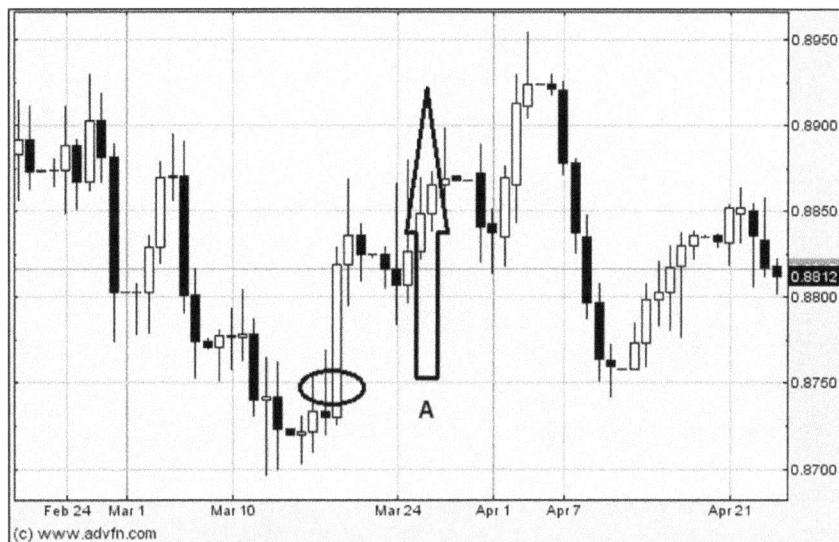

[Chart Key:

A = The US's Fed Chair, Janet Yellen, indicates that the longstanding target of the Fed before it can raise interest rates – 6.5% or less unemployment – has been discarded, prompting markets to anticipate earlier US rates rises, and more of them, than it had done; hence, more CHF-funded USD buying]

The 'carry' effect is even more pronounced on one of the most longstanding of this type of trade: the long AUDJPY position, despite the negative fallout for Australia of concerns over the rate of China's future growth (China has accounted for around 30%-40% of all Australia's exports, principally commodities, for the past few years).

AUDJPY (6 Months, Daily)

Once the current wave of monetary expansion (principally QE programmes) looks like it is coming to an end – as has already been signalled by the Fed – then **interest rate differentials between currencies will widen further as several other major central banks allow themselves to shift to a more hawkish interest rate policy. This increases rate differentials once again and further improves the return on carry exposures.**

Having said that, as mentioned earlier, for a prevalent carry trading paradigm to re-establish itself, FX volatilities need to be low enough to avoid wiping out the interest rate gain with currency losses. In this respect there is some divergence in interpreting the headline volatility numbers.

In this respect, although FX volatilities have fallen substantially in recent years – on the surface to around pre-financial crisis levels (see above chart) – their trajectory is far from certain, given a range of metrics.

To begin with, only a very limited number of variables do a good job of explaining realised volatility across most exchange rates, including the US unemployment rate, US industrial production, changes in commodity prices and equity valuations.

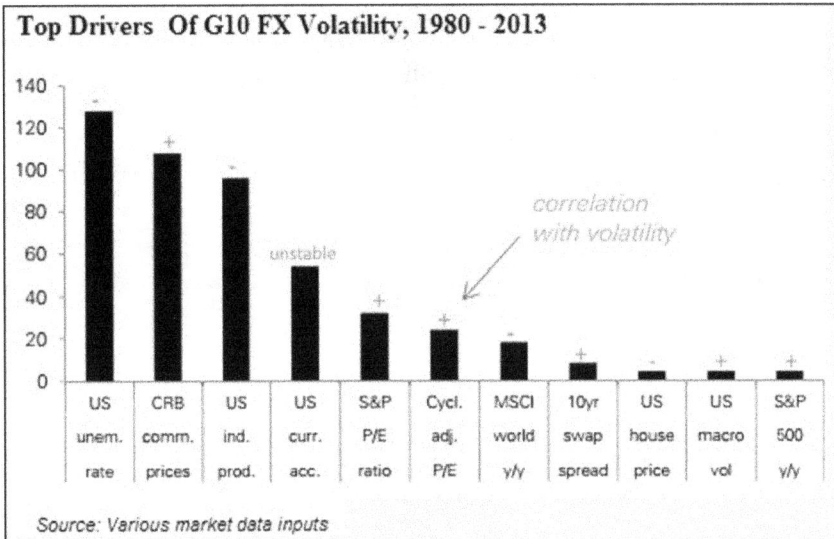

Top Drivers Of G10 FX Volatility, 1980 - 2013

correlation with volatility

unstable

| US unem. rate | CRB comm. prices | US ind. prod. | US curr. acc. | S&P P/E ratio | Cycl. adj. P/E | MSCI world y/y | 10yr swap spread | US house price | US macro vol | S&P 500 y/y |

Source: Various market data inputs

For the past few months, better growth or higher commodity prices have lowered volatility, but higher stock market valuations have been associated with higher volatility. Better current accounts in the US and Europe have also lowered realised volatility, although this signal has been unreliable across other currencies.

These results make perfect sense, of course, given that weaker growth is in general associated with higher policy uncertainty and investor deleveraging, which in turn should lead to higher volatility down the line.

Certainly it is wise to bear in mind generally that **carry crosses rally in a low-vol trend as confidence improves, but the unwind is sharper and more disorderly when confidence deteriorates.**

Carry, of course, is just one of the key non-long only (moronic) trading strategies, the others being: 'momentum' (used when an asset is moving firmly and persistently in one direction, as we saw with the yen for while, as shown above); 'value', a variant of 'mean reversion' (when an asset is above or below what is considered to be 'fair value', classically as determined by its relation to PPP, as would be the case with sterling if it were not for the troubles affecting the other three major SDR currencies); and, pure 'volatility' plays (these should be left alone by the inexperienced retail trader, as highlighted later in this book).

Range Of Basic Investment Styles For FX And Commodities Trading

	MOMENTUM Persistence in asset returns	CARRY Higher yielding assets tend to outperform	VALUE Assets below "fair-value" outperform	VOLATILITY Option sellers earn "insurance" premia
G10 FX *	Buy (sell) currency when past performance is strong (weak)	Buy (sell) currencies when interest rates are high (low)	Buy (sell) currencies based on under (over)-valuation relative to PPP	Sell delta-hedged ATM straddles
Commodities **	Buy (sell) commodities when past performance is strong (weak)	Buy (sell) commodities in backwardation (contango)	Buy (sell) commodities which are under (over) valued	-
EM FX ***	Buy (sell) currency when past performance is strong (weak)	Buy (sell) currencies when interest rates are high (low)	-	-

* USD, EUR, GBP, JPY, CHF, CAD, AUD, NZD, NOK and SEK

** WTI Crude, Brent Crude, Heating Oil, Gasoline, Gas Oil, Natural Gas, Gold, Silver, Copper, Aluminium, Zinc, Nickel, Lead, Corn, Soybean, Wheat, Sugar, Coffee, Cocoa, Cotton, Live Cattle and Lean Hogs

*** BRL, CNY, INR, KRW, MXN, PLN, RUB, SGD, TRY and ZAR

PPP = Purchasing Power Parity

Source: Various

Momentum Trading

As mentioned above, low volatility in markets is no bar to making serious money, and momentum trading is one trading style that particularly benefits in such dealing conditions. The beauty of this in a low volatility environment is that you can stick a trade on and not worry too much about getting stopped out on the other side through wild price swings.

Many currencies have exhibited straightforward momentum (up or down) in recent low volatility periods: GBP, EUR and the JPY are three of the majors that particularly spring to mind in this context, generally strengthening in the case of the first two and broadly weakening in the case of the latter. We will have a look at all three, based against the USD as a control currency, to see how the momentum has manifested itself very clearly.

EURUSD (1 Year, Daily, With MACD Underchart)

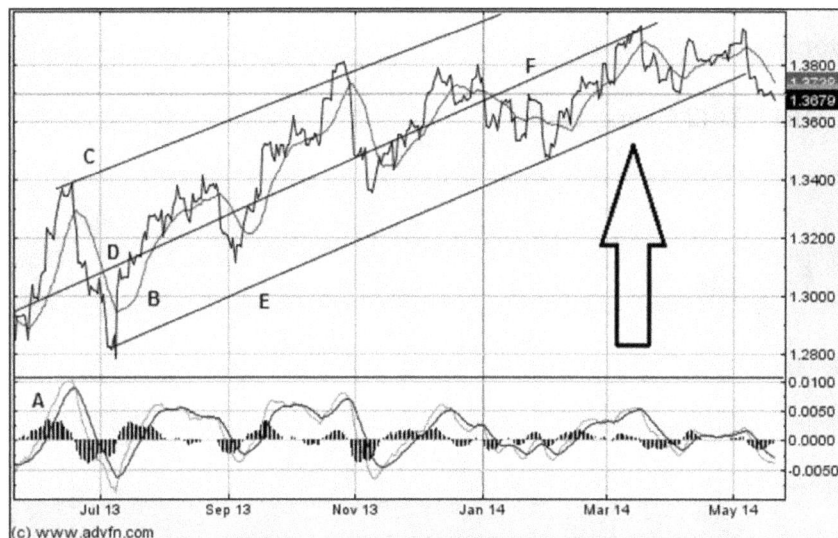

[Chart Key:
A = Moving Average Convergence Divergence indicator clearly shows some divergence from the overall unidirectional trend of the EUR strengthening against the USD
B = Simple Moving Average indicator reiterates small divergence from the overall EUR strengthening trend
C = Upper (resistance) price band
D = Middle price route
E = Lower (support) price band
F = Overall upwards price trend]

There were sound fundamental and technical reasons for buying euros against US dollars at the time (i.e. ongoing US QE weakening the USD, central banks reweighting reserves in favour of the EUR etc), so the key to putting the trade on would have been selection of the levels (*see Technical Analysis section on page 137*).

To do this, as mentioned in *Looking At Different Time Periods Of Charts* on page 12, you would need to go back as far as possible and look at the support levels (as you are a buyer) in order to select your stop-loss on your long.

EURUSD (2 Years, Daily)

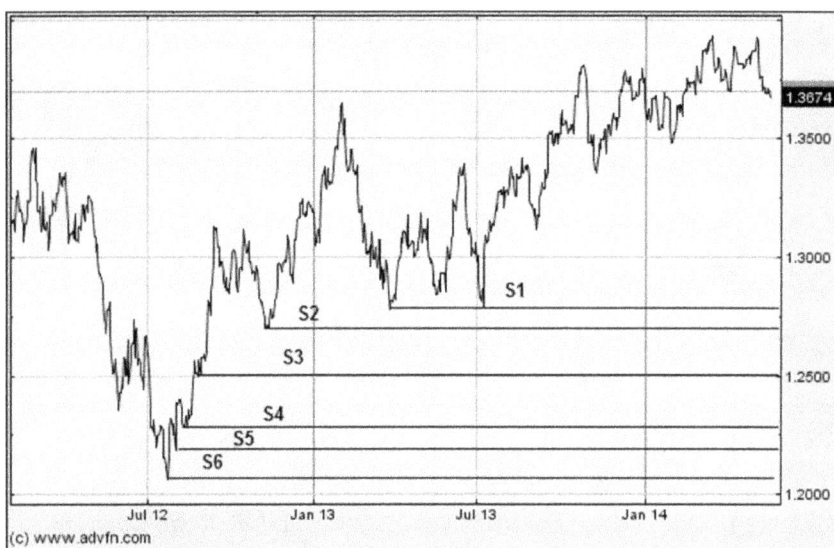

[*Chart Key:*
S1 – S6 = Declining support levels]

As can be seen in the chart above, the natural base of EURUSD over the previous two years was 1.2050, BUT more importantly, as that level looked a thing of the dim and distant past for the time being, there was a double support level more recently at 1.2780, so, as EURUSD continued to move in its upwards momentum corridor, that would have been an ideal stop loss level.

Therefore, one would have been looking out for an upside break to indicate that upwards momentum was still on track, and the natural resistance point would have been as shown below.

EURUSD (2 Years, Daily)

(c) www.advfn.com

[Chart Key:
A to D = quadruple recent major resistance level]

So, with the fundamentals in place (see above) and ready to take a long EURUSD, the break at the quadruple resistance level at 1.3110 would be a great place to buy euros, with a stop at the previously mentioned super-support level of 1.2780, which would be a downside of 330 pips.

The upside target would be four times that, at least, which is entirely realistic, based on previous resistance levels, as shown below.

EURUSD (6 Years, Weekly)

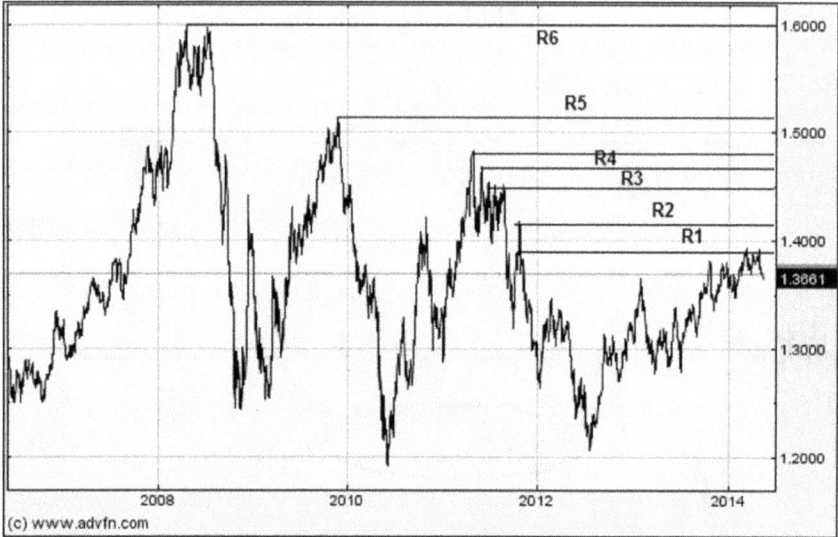

(c) www.advfn.com

[Chart Key:
R1 to R6 = Previous major resistance levels]

Consequently, the trade now looks like this:

Buy EURUSD GBP10 per pip @ 1.3110, stop loss @ 1.2780

Initial Take-Profit Target = 1.4490 (1,380 pips upside)

Risk/Reward Ratio = 4X

Profit = GBP13,800

In the interim, one can take part-profit at the R1 level, of 780 pips, or work trailing stop losses (*see page 112, Risk Management section*).

By the way, for shorter views on momentum-based trading strategies, ADVFN has introduced a useful indicator *'Forex Scope'*; if you are using it make sure that you keep snapshots of it on a daily basis to glean the rolling full picture.

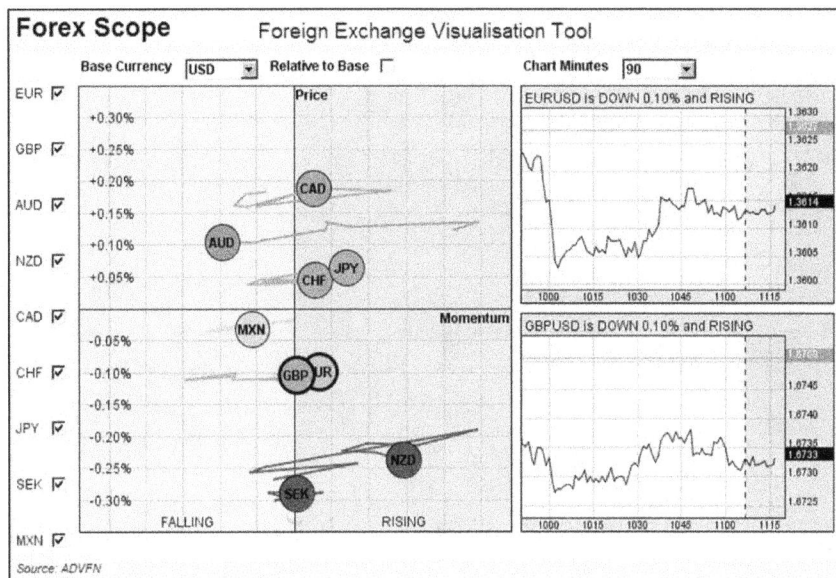

Source: ADVFN

Value Trading

In classical terms, this is determined by a currency's relation to Purchasing Power Parity (PPP). This means that two currencies will find an equilibrium point at a level where the same product/service costs the same in each country, having taken into account the exchange rate.

A commonly used example of this is the McDonalds' 'Big Mac', as the usually redoubtable 'Economist' magazine regularly published its 'Big Mac Index' for precisely the reason of discerning correct PPPs.

So, for example, if a Big Mac costs USD2 in the US and GBP1 in Great Britain then the exchange rate should be, according to the PPP measure, GBP1:USD2. The PPP, then, reflects inflationary data, as if the Consumer Price Index (CPI) inflation measure went up in Great

Britain to a degree that it now cost GBP2 for a Big Mac then the exchange rate would be parity between the two currencies – that is, GBP1:USD1.

For the purposes of this trading style, though, we are just going to consider it in terms of value in the sense of averages, which in this context indicates 'mean reversion' trading.

For example: where should the JPY be trading compared to the US dollar?

USDJPY (2 Years, Daily)

[Chart Key:
A = Despite ongoing economic stagnation, JPY buying from speculative funds keeps US JPY around the 75.00 level, damaging Japan's economy further
B = After Shinzo Abe becomes PM, a new economic policy pushes the JPY weaker
C = Doubts about the sustainability of Abe's new economic policy overtakes the JPY, causing stasis]

Below highlights the difficulty in undertaking real value trading, aside from implementing proxy mean reversion techniques:

USDJPY(1972-2014)

Source: Trading Economics

It could be argued that there has been no seismic shift in Japan's economy to warrant a move in true value from USDJPY300 to USD100 from 1972 to currently, and the chances of USDJPY reverting to anywhere near to pure mean average middle point of 200 remains in the realms of the extremely unlikely.

Looking though at closer timeframes and trading back to the mean provides ample scope for repeated and reliable profits, especially when overlain with a momentum trade dimension.

Basic Ongoing Momentum Trade

Long USDJPY on fundamentals (change in economic policy, under new PM, with integrated JPY weakness) as USDJPY breaks major resistance at 83.25, GBP10 per pip, and stop loss at 82.15 support level downside risk is 110 pips.

USDJPY (2 Years, Daily)

[Chart Key:
A = Outer price band
B = Middle price band
C = Lower price band
D = USDJPY stasis as Abe economic policy sustainability is questioned
E = Major previous resistance level]

The obvious target here, for technical and fundamental reasons, is 100. **Therefore, the momentum side profit of this trade would have been GBP16,750, with a Risk/Reward ratio of over 10X.**

However, **playing the mean reversion trades all the way up would have exponentially increased your profits**, as shown in the simplified example below.

USDJPY (2 Years, Daily)

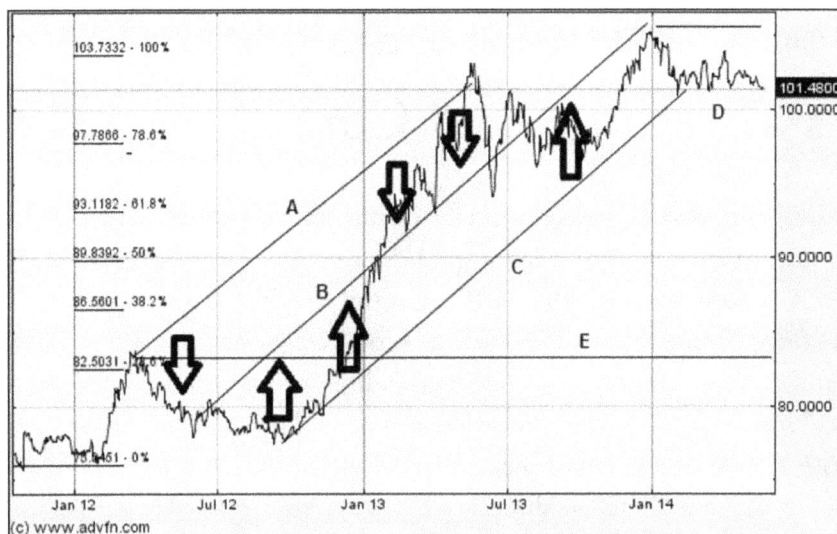

The above is a very long-term view, but exactly the same can be done utilising Moving Averages (Simple, Exponential etc) and Bollinger Bands, in tandem with other indicators. For a much more detailed discussion of how to use these, please see the *Technical Analysis* section on page 137.

Risk-On/Risk-Off
Trading And Correlations

As I have tried to stress before, **jobbing in and out of an asset in isolation in search of a few pips here and there is a mug's game. It is a key reason why 90% of retail traders lose all of their dealing money within 90 days.** Not being one of these – and, rather, being one of those that makes life-changing serious money – requires self-discipline, knowledge of trading fundamentals (see earlier), a sound grasp of technical analysis and risk management (see later) and the ability to discern what patterns are in play across the global financial markets. This last point is what this section is about.

In general terms, the degree to which the price action of all major financial markets assets are correlated positively or negatively has varied since this phenomenon fully manifested itself after the collapse of Lehman Brothers in 2008. It is equally the case, though, that **these correlations, which are a function of the risk of systemic failure across the global financial system, remain a significant common price component of all assets in all regions across the world.**

When the risk of this failure rises there is a shift towards less risk-exposed assets ('risk off') and when it falls there is a move towards more risk-exposed assets ('risk on'); both conditions together being acronymically termed 'RORO'. Either way, the fact that the prices of apparently disparate individual assets move in tandem (either positively correlated or inversely correlated) means that **classical methods of maximising returns whilst minimising risk will remain sidelined for the foreseeable future, calling for shrewder and nimbler investment approaches going forward.**

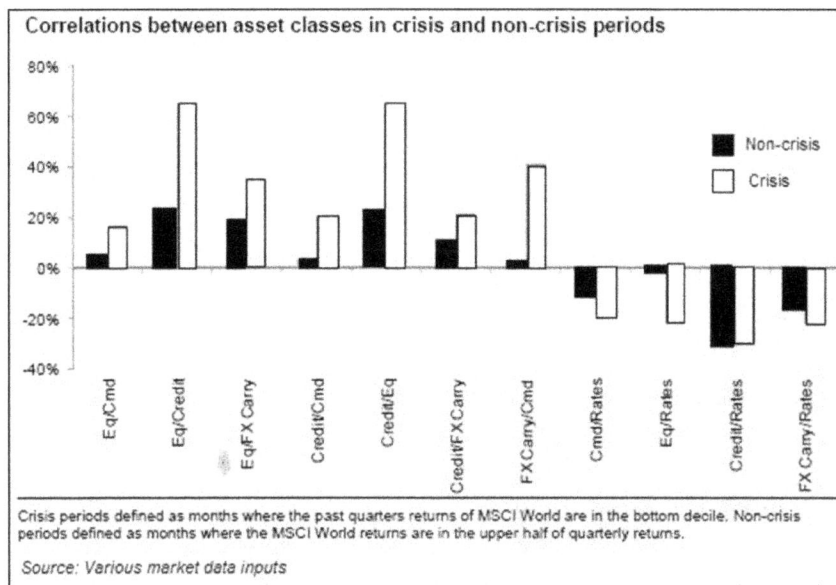

Correlations between asset classes in crisis and non-crisis periods

Crisis periods defined as months where the past quarters returns of MSCI World are in the bottom decile. Non-crisis periods defined as months where the MSCI World returns are in the upper half of quarterly returns.

Source: Various market data inputs

The notion that different regions, asset classes and market types (developed or emerging) are driven in large part by their own fundamentals, and that consequently diversification of risk can be achieved by investing cross-regionally, cross-asset class and cross market-type, or any combination thereof, weighted appropriately, remains largely redundant during many market periods.

A more nuanced approach is now generally required: for example, 2013 started out looking risk-on but with the distinct potential for temporary risk-off conditions being triggered by political concerns, in the eurozone periphery in particular.

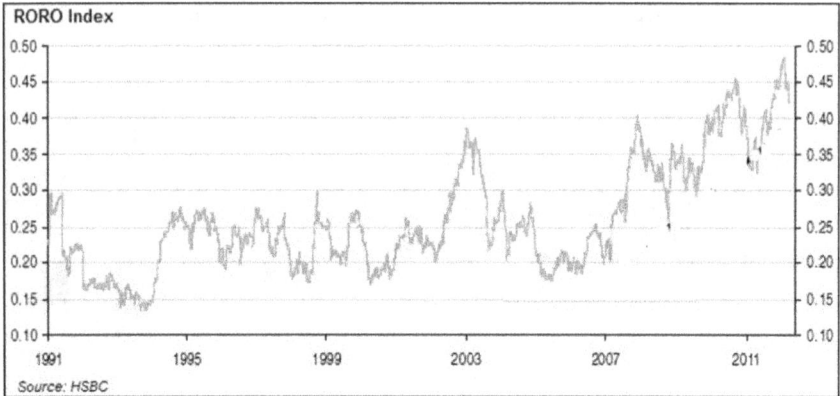

RORO Index

Source: HSBC

Consequently, at that time, one might prefer a higher allocation to cash instead of holding any government bonds or related developed market currencies, and then a risk-weighted allocation to exposures such as equities, emerging market currencies and selected commodities that are likely to respond well to risk-on environments.

This might be considered a bar-bell approach to risk/return, with the former flight to quality exposures in government bonds being sized to zero in favour of more cash and an appropriately sized allocation to riskier exposures.

This said, the **idea of what may be classed as 'safe-haven' assets or 'risky' ones has changed much in a short time and continues to do so at a fast pace** (by the way, many banks and trading platforms issue 'heatmaps' of changing correlations, but HSBC's is always especially good).

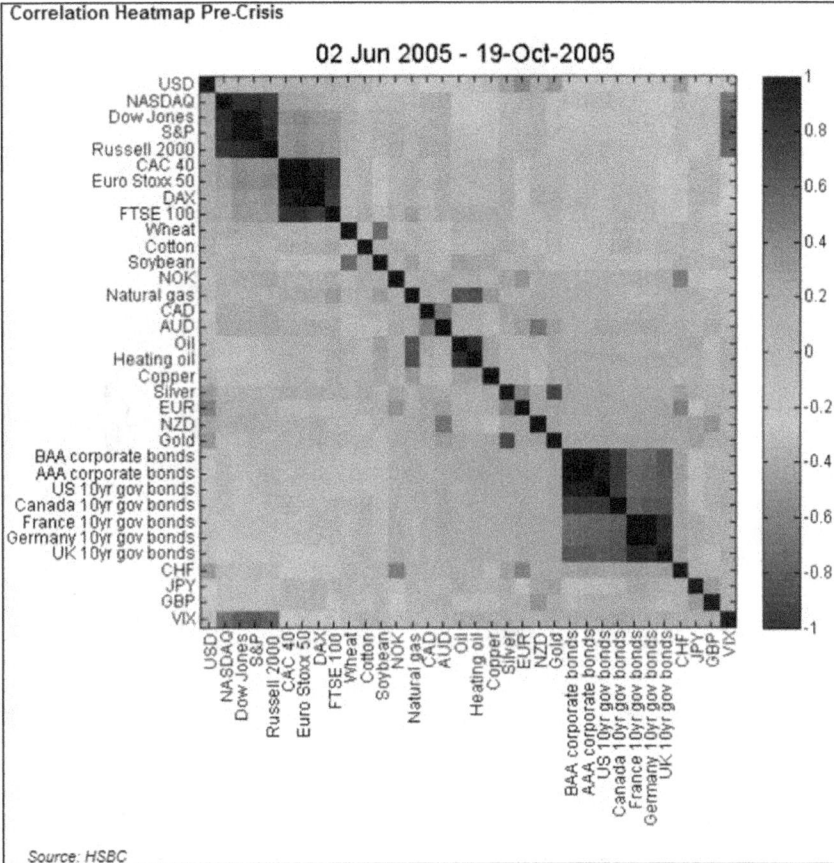

Correlation Heatmap Pre-Crisis

02 Jun 2005 - 19-Oct-2005

Source: HSBC

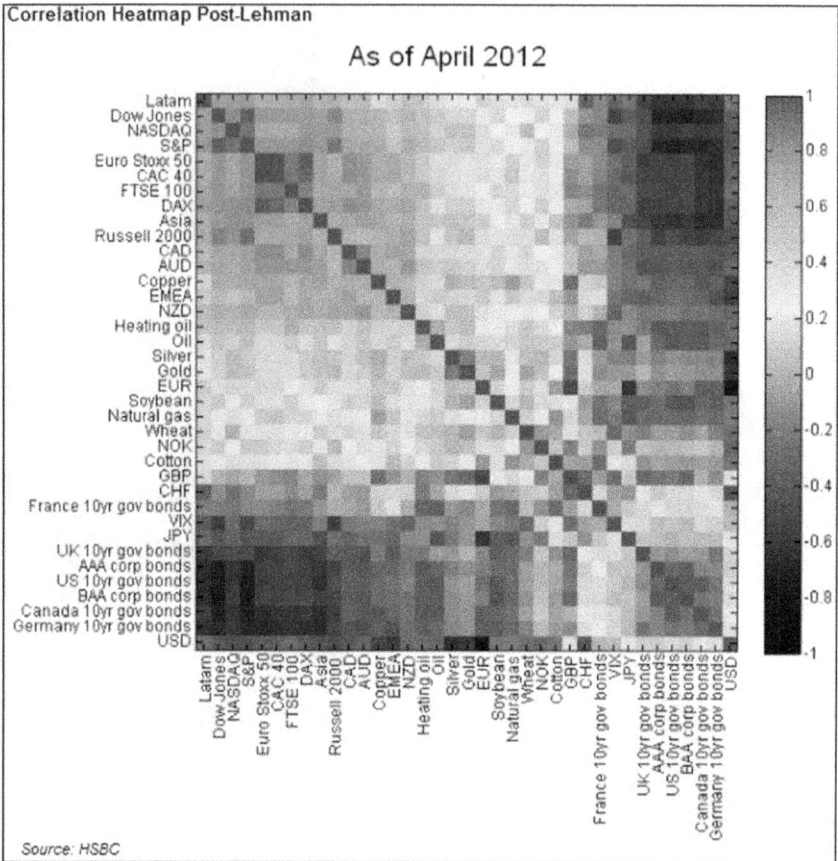

Correlation Heatmap Post-Lehman

As of April 2012

Source: HSBC

Risk-On Assets

In broad terms, the most risk on assets remain equities. The S&P500 is consistently the most risk-on asset over time, with a natural adjunct high-risk asset being the Dow Jones Industrial Average, DJIA. Asia and Latin America swap places as the most risky of emerging markets in general and US 10-year government bonds generally occupy the least risky position on the correlations matrix.

In practical terms, then, **when risk is perceived to rise across global markets, selling the Dow is usually a winner,** as can be seen below in a small-scale example when international political tensions rose as Russia ramped up its threats against the new government in Ukraine, after the removal of Russia's man in Kiev, former President Viktor Yanukovych.

Dow Jones Industrial Average (6 Months, Daily)

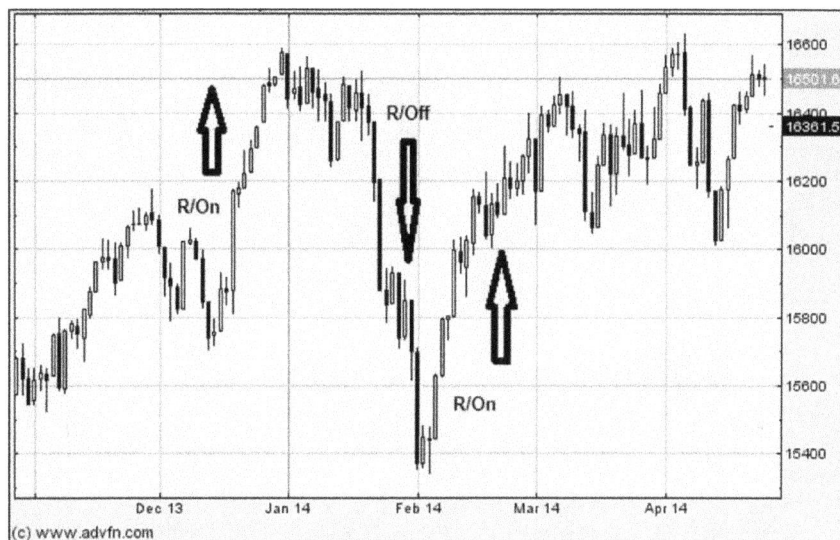

[Chart Key:
First R/On from left to right = Market volatility is low, volumes as well, as Christmas approaches
R/Off = Ukraine President and Russia's man in the country, Viktor Yanukovych, is overthrown, global political tensions rise and Russia annexes Crimea
Second R/On = Russia halts military action for a while after Crimea votes to ally with Russia]

Going short the Dow when the tension started to really mount, at around 16,500 at GBP10 per pip, would have netted a straight

1,000 pip profit in around a couple of weeks: that is, around GBP10,000.

Again, in general terms, the AUD, CAD and NZD are consistently regarded as the riskiest of the developed markets' currencies, whilst **the CHF is always seen as the least risky** (principally because it has all the benefits of a European trading and banking location without all of the interminable disaster politics connected to the euro).

This latter correlation was **perfectly highlighted again during the Russia/Ukraine mini-crisis** as described above, as shown in the chart below.

USDCHF (6 Months, Daily)

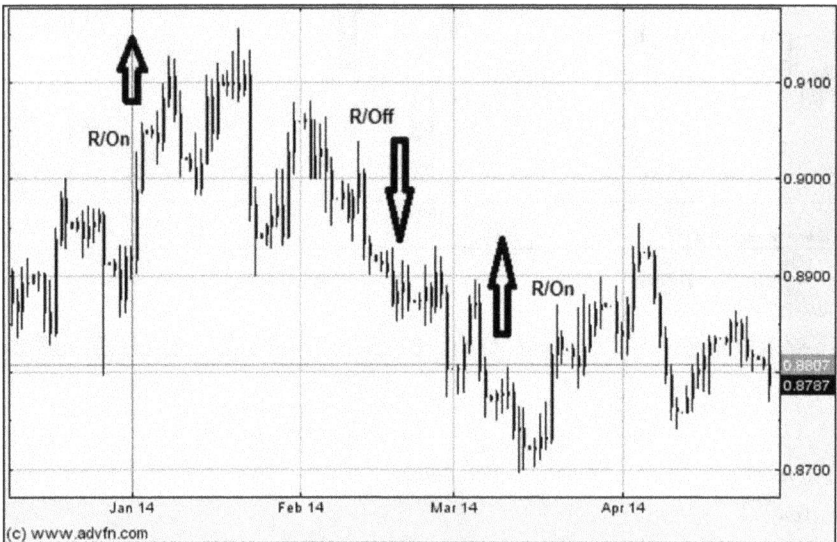

[Chart Key:
R/On = Risk-on
R/Off = Risk-off]

Risk-Off Assets (And Pure Safe-Havens)

In the above, **perfectly mirroring the performance of the Dow, the CHF** weakened against the USD during the pre-Christmas 2014 Risk-On period and then strengthened markedly against it as global risk rose during the Russia/Ukraine mini-crisis, only to re-establish a Risk-On pattern as those risks, temporarily at least, diminished.

Had one traded exclusively according to RORO principles then the trades would have been as follows:

First R/On Period = Long USDCHF GBP10 per pip @ 0.8820, stop loss @ 0.8790 (good historical support, maximum loss = GBP300), sell @ 0.9100 (strong resistance) = GBP1800 profit

R/Off Period = Short USDCHF GBP10 per pip @ 0.9100, stop loss 0.9130 (maximum loss = GBP300), target = 0.8760 (strong USD support previously), buy back @ 0.8760 = GBP3,400 profit

Total Profit, without Second R/On Period included = GBP5,200

Commodities In The RORO Mix

Commodities had, and still have, clear correlations for FX of which traders should be aware. Of course, commodities can also be traded over many electronic dealing platforms, as well as through Exchange Traded Funds (ETFs).

Twenty years ago, it seemed that there were fairly clear principles for investors to follow: for instance, the higher the crude oil price, the higher the USD; the greater the economic growth in China, the greater base metals' prices; and the more political uncertainties in key global powers, the more the gold

price would rise, to name but three. Around ten years ago these altered slightly, and after 2008 they switched again.

Gold And FX

Looking at the latter first, there was a general view that gold was a usual beneficiary of heightened risk across the globe, on the basis that, unlike currencies, more cannot simply be produced at the drop of a central bank's printing presses (as in QE).

So, for example, the correlations for gold were fairly simple: if the USD looked weak, then gold would be strong.

However, gold trading patterns over recent years are instructive of a number of factors that will determine the trading trajectories going forward not just of this metal, but of silver and the better-traded platinum group metals (PGMs, including platinum and palladium).

For a start, gold had been regarded as the archetypal 'safe-haven' commodities asset in times of political uncertainty (troubles in the Middle East, for example, sparking buying not just in that area but around the globe), in the same way that the Swiss franc is seen as such in currency terms.

Additionally, it has been seen as a hedge against inflation concerns that have risen sharply on the basis of the QE policies adopted by the Fed, the BOJ, the ECB (long-term refinancing operations (LTRO) was QE by another name) and until recently the BOE as well.

Gold (USD, Comex, 5 Years, Weekly, Elided)

By both of these principles, though, there was no clearly defined reason for the recent massive sustained drop in gold prices. The BOE was for a long time more likely than not to re-embark on QE, given the failure of the UK government to engender meaningful economic growth, as was the ECB with its LTRO, or via direct bond-buying, like the Fed. The BOJ was duty bound to continue with its QE and associated monetary easing programs until it attains its two key targets of 2% inflation per year and a 3% nominal GDP rate, and the Fed itself only began to taper its QE programme at the end of 2013.

Not just this, but interest rates in all key global centres not only showed no signs of moving up for a very long period since 2007/08 but rather had a risk further to the downside, both highlighting the lack of inflationary expectations in them and also lowering the relative return on cash holdings over gold from interest rate rewards.

It was, instead, a unique combination of factors that pushed gold down so precipitously, along with silver and the well-traded PGMs–critically aligned with the means of trade execution.

To begin with, the 10 April 2013 **US FOMC minutes** highlighted that some members of the committee favour an early end to the country's QE programme, so reducing the inflation 'safe-haven' argument for some who held gold. There was also a statement on 9 April by the European Commission (EC) that **Cyprus** had committed to selling about EUR400mn (USD525mn) of "excess" gold reserves to help ease its debt situation. Whilst not a huge amount, it sparked the notion that lots of other indebted countries might follow suit and sell their gold reserves as well. **Technically also, once key support levels were broken** (USD1525/Oz, 1505.00 and 1500.00) then the inevitable large stop loss selling occurred and developed as it always does a momentum of its own. And then there was an extra spark igniting this bonfire of uncertainty, which was large 'guru' investment firms issuing sell signals on the metals.

The key point here, though, was the disproportionate effect that the selling of relatively small quantities of gold through Exchange Traded Funds (ETFs), in comparison with the market in general, had on the precious metals prices. In this respect, robust investor appetite for gold ETFs had been an important ingredient in gold's rally since 2004, and at their height gold ETFs held the equivalent of around 90% of annual mine supply at the end of 2012.

Although the bulk of ETF investors – including pension funds, real asset managers and high net worth retail individuals – have a 'buy and hold' trading strategy **it is clear that hedge fund liquidation has noticeably reduced ETF holdings and, given the size of the ETFs, the potential for further liquidation exists. Should liquidation continue, it is likely to be from macro hedge funds,**

and hedge fund liquidation is fast whilst real economy buying is slow.

There is another key point here, which pertains to the increased policy remits of central banks that I mentioned earlier, and it is vital in understanding that buying and selling gold on dealing platforms is not as straightforward a play as one might think.

The thing is that for a long time now, ever since interest rates in the major economies plummeted to settle near to, or at, zero, in fact, **major central banks have been selling gold on bounces in order to discourage investors from selling the currencies of those central banks (USD, EUR and GBP to name but three) in order to switch to gold;** simple as that.

Interestingly, and a vital point for those looking to trade the metals complex, especially gold, is that certain central banks have employed dealing tactics usually associated with hedge funds, whilst hedge funds themselves have traded as they always do, and it's worth noting what typical tactics are, in order that you can trade along with them (in circumstances like this, it is relatively easy money).

Gold (USD, Comex, 2 Years, Weekly)

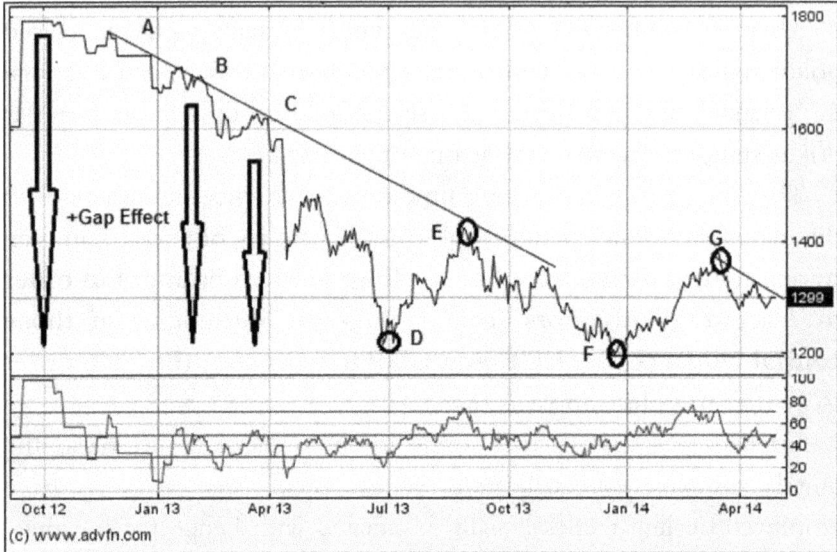

[Chart Key:

A = HFs and Central Banks (CBs) sell at key technical resistance level, 1795.00

B = HFs and CBs sell again at next major technical level, 1765.00

C = HFs and CBs sell again at next major technical level, 1725.00

D = HFs part buy back shorts aggressively

E = CBs cap buying again, 1425.00

F = HFs part buy back shorts aggressively, 1195.00

G = CBs cap buying again, 1380.00

Therefore, CBs establish a temporary trading range of 1195.00-1425.00]

The above chart shows a number of key facets of hedge fund and new central bank trading of which the retail trader needs to be aware. To begin with, it is wise to note that whatever the underlying rationale behind the trade may well have been, **hedge funds and the central banks nowadays will add dynamic and aggressive intraday trading tactics** to the mix.

In the above example, for instance, **most of the major moves happen overnight or in other periods in which the market is relatively illiquid. This was, and is, a classic hedge fund strategy and now is one shared by the central banks**. It means that less money can have a disproportionately greater effect on the price than in normal liquid conditions.

Another tactic frequently employed by hedge funds, and now the central banks, is to **trend the market in one direction, encouraging others (especially retail traders) to follow that trend and then to rapidly square off that position and simultaneously take the opposite one, so triggering extra stop-loss action** (in this case, selling of gold).

In this instance, those retail traders who did not read top-notch market analysis and monitor trading flows would have found their long gold positions going quickly against them and then being stopped out (i.e. having to sell out their longs). Add in all of these RT stops going through the market in illiquid conditions and the stage had been set for a rapid move back down, which is exactly what the hedge funds and central banks wanted in the above example.

A final point of which to be aware is **that hedge funds and central banks often choose to launch such ambushes at key technical levels** (see combined *Risk Management and Technical Analysis sections* of this book, pages 112 and 137 respectively) where they know RT investors will be watching closely for directional signs: hence, in the above example, selling at major resistance levels, Fibonacci retracements and so forth. However, it is important to note that hedge funds in particular often choose to reverse these positions at levels which apparently have no technical significance whatsoever, thus taking everyone by surprise and hijacking market momentum.

Finally, remember that once hedge funds and the central banks get it into their collective minds to go after something that they want one way or another then there is little any other trader can do to alter their path, so hop on board the ride, if you think the move is genuine.

In the above example, for instance, had one simply copied the trades and direction of the hedge funds and central banks then the rewards would have been staggering. This can be found in the **'Commitment of Traders Report'** (COT), which is available for free on the **Commodities Futures Trading Commission** (CFTC) website (http://www.cmegroup.com/trading/fx/cftc-tff/main.html) and although this is data that applies specifically to the futures market, it is equally applicable to sentiment in the spot FX market and other asset markets, including commodities, and it is updated every Friday.

Gold (USD, Comex, 2 Years, Weekly)

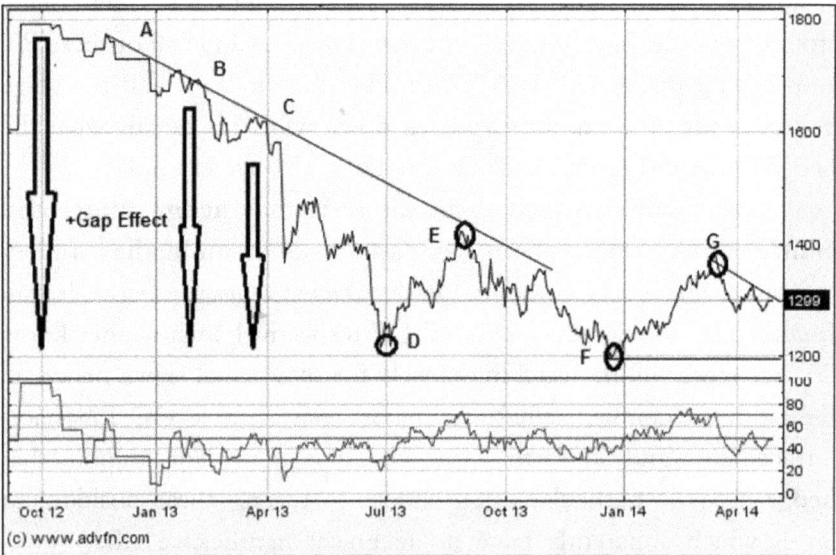

[Chart Key: Gold Tandem Trade With The CBs And HFs:
A = Short GBP10 per pip @ 1795.00
B = Short GBP10 per pip @ 1765.00
C = Short GBP10 per pip @ 1725.00

D = Buy back shorts @ double support on 1215.00

Total Profit = GBP1,181,000 (yes, you read it right; that is over one million pounds profit)].

Regulatory Change That Favours Gold Going Forward

That the gold price is subject to intense and concerted manipulation (downwards) by key central banks would seem to be a truism.

In 2012, for example, actual gold demand was USD236.4bn – an all-time high, according to the World Gold Council's full year 2012 *'Gold Demand Trends'* report. In Q4 alone, demand in value terms was 6% higher year-on-year (y/y), at USD66.2bn, marking the highest ever Q4 total.

Looking more specifically behind the headline numbers, while Indian full year demand was down 12% y/y and Chinese demand was flat year-on-year, overall central bank buying for the full year rose by 17% y/y, totalling 534.6t, the highest level since 1964. Additionally, global investment in ETFs in 2012 was up by 51% y/y.

Moreover, a profoundly important regulatory change also came into effect as from 1 January 2013 with the introduction of the Basel III directive, in conjunction with various other changes to the global regulatory investment framework.

In this context, **the Basel Committee on Banking Supervision changed the rules on what can be used as collateral in investments and how much collateral any item can be used as. And, in this respect, gold could be used as collateral on a 1:1 basis (called Tier 1 capital) and not on a 1:2 basis (Tier 3 capital as it was before).**

So, to put it simply, whereas before if a bank was going to buy a USD1mn house through debt then it would have to put up USD2mn worth of gold, from 2013 it would only have to put up USD1mn worth of gold. Gold, therefore, was from that point to be considered on a par with actual cash.

So, why was it capped? As I mentioned before, the key reason was to dissuade investors from liquidating their holdings in key troubled currencies – thus exacerbating existing market jitteriness in those currencies – by the relevant central banks.

Additionally, of course, was **good old manipulation of a market that is characterised by being a 'zero-sum game'** (one investor winning means another will lose) where, given the new collateral requirements as outlined above, other central banks wanted to buy in their gold as cheaply as possible.

The same trick is used across all markets, most recently in the oil market (although this investigation has apparently stalled in its tracks) and involves an investor (in this case, central banks) buying up a commodity in the spot market, whilst selling it further forward to reduce market expectations of a continued rise in price (contango market, that is, rising over time) which, in turn, feeds back into the spot price.

As we touched on the oil price, the trick is shorter-term but of the same type. Investors need to be aware of this, as it is a very good reason to remain broadly long oil, provided political risks (such as we saw a while back with increased tension over Iran, which controls the Strait of Hormuz through which about 20% or the world's petroleum and about 35% of the petroleum traded by sea passes) do not rise precipitously.

The trick here is: buy as much physical crude oil as possible in the spot market, store it in tankers and also buy oil futures, creating a contango market. When the time comes, sell the physical oil stored on the tankers into the market for a guaranteed profit: simple, but extremely effective.

In terms of the oil price/USD relationship, this remained unusual for a very long period. A while back, the consensus was that there was a directly proportionate relation between real oil prices and the dollar (the higher the oil price the higher the dollar, basically).

The idea behind this was that as oil prices rose then the demand for dollars to buy it would increase and thus the USD would strengthen.

Over the past 10 years or so, this relationship completely broke down, as rising oil prices coincided with a broadly weaker dollar. And this was explained by the idea that rising oil prices led to deterioration in the US trade deficit (oil and oil products represent around 50% of the entire US trade deficit).

Other Metals

Unlike gold, other metals are subject less to the straightforward 'investment' arguments – and thus the same dramatic whipsawing in price that we saw with gold in the past couple of years or so – than to a combination of 'investment plus industrial utility' rationales.

Silver, for example, whilst having an element of gold's 'store of value' notion attached to it, is also used in consumer products (increasing global use of cell phones and computers has sparked greater demand for silver, and its high resistance to heat and the highest electrical conductivity of any element makes it good in televisions and batteries). Indeed, around half of all of the metal's demand comes from such uses in industry.

For the PGMs, **platinum is barely viewed as an investment asset at all, principally because there is so little of it physically that it makes electronic trading in the metal a much more difficult prospect than gold**. Indeed, of the 245 tonnes or so of platinum sold in 2012, 113 tonnes were used for vehicle emissions control devices (46%), 76 tonnes for jewellery (31%), whilst the remainder went in various other minor applications, such as investment, electrodes, anti-cancer drugs, oxygen sensors, spark plugs and turbine engines. Its PGM counterpart, in the meantime, palladium, is 60% utilised in the automotive industry (in catalytic converters).

One interesting point of which to be aware when trading gold and platinum (again, the latter is offered over a range of trading platforms nowadays) is that **historically platinum has usually commanded a premium correlation to gold of around USD200-400/Oz or so, giving regular opportunities for divergence trading**.

Gold and Platinum Correlation (1 Year, Daily)

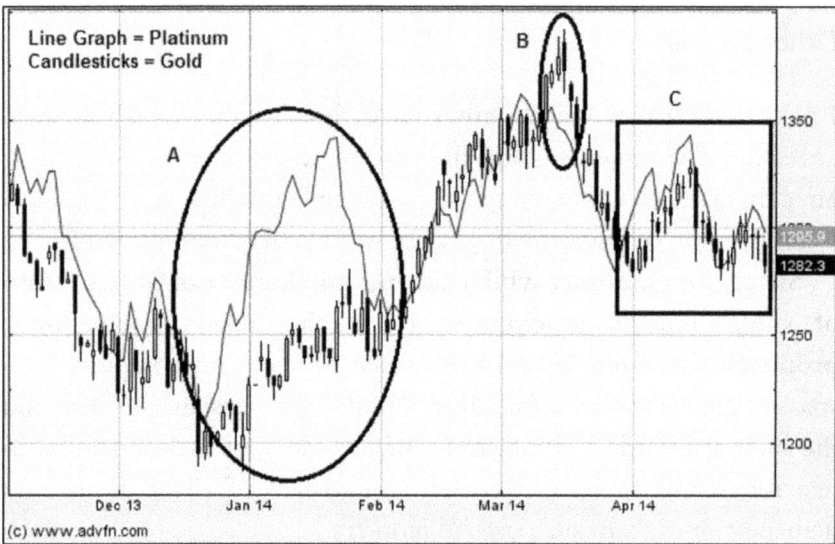

[Chart Key:
A = Usual premium of platinum to gold re-established as RORO profile allows fundamentals to come back to the fore
B = For only one of a handful of occasions in the past 25 years, the gold price overtakes that of platinum, opening up a sell gold, buy platinum trade]
C = Gold/platinum price near convergence as both are seen in the same Risk-On trading environment]

Had one used this gold/platinum divergence signal as another confirmation for a short gold position, then the trade would have been:

Sell gold, GBP10 per pip, at 1390.00 (previous strong resistance level, stop loss at 1395, sell as platinum and gold converge at 1280.00 = **Total Profit of GBP110,000.**

For these metals, then, and for the major base metals – copper, iron ore, aluminium, zinc – and for crude oil to a lesser directly proportionate degree (as it is also USD-trend related, but inversely proportionate now), **the argument for future investment trajectories becomes less directly about expectations for inflation, interest rates and FX levels and more about growth prospects in key markets, especially China, and then about supply projections to meet that growth (more of this later).**

In this context, **China has accounted for around 50% of the world's total demand for all base metals and around 20% of its energy demand in the past ten years, but over that period the country's growth was heavily skewed towards manufacturing and infrastructure development, whereas in the most recent five year economic plan it has shifted its growth strategy towards being more consumer-led.**

This explains why there has been a **broad-based tightening of the correlation between all commodities prices in general (as shown on the Goldman Sachs Commodities Index, GSCI) and the Purchasing Managers Index (PMI)** – for both manufacturing and for services – coming out of China in the past few months.

Indeed, the PMIs seem to point not necessarily to a hard landing for China, but certainly to a soft one that is not being driven by resource-intensive growth, such as building bridges, motorways, hospitals and so on; so, whereas we had a metals upwards pricing supercycle for a long while, cycles only work well in a manufacturing-based economy and not in a services-based one.

Added to these factors, **there is one other that militates against a long-ranging rebound for commodities as a group: in an investment world dominated by a search for yield, commodities** not only yield nothing whatsoever, but actually cost investors money to hold.

Correlations Are Constantly Shifting

Within these broad sweeps of what's regarded as 'safe' or 'risky', though, major realignments occur and therein even more money lies. For instance, two years ago – despite ongoing problems with the eurozone – French government bonds (and to a lesser degree those of Italy) fell within the safe-haven category, but then, as the vicious bailout of Cyprus reignited fears over a run on eurozone banks, both shifted markedly into the 'risk on' investment profile, as the markets looked for the most vulnerable assets to the bloc's possible contagion.

In a similar vein, a long USD-denominated oil position is really a relative-value trade between oil and the USD, as oil priced in AUD and CAD – at least at the moment – is much less RORO-dominated and more likely to respond more cleanly to oil-specific fundamentals.

Similarly, the notion that developed markets' longer-dated bonds (and by extension, their currencies, as bonds are largely just an FX proxy in many market circumstances) are safe-havens again does not bear up to closer examination from a serious investor perspective.

It is true that US bonds have always figured on the safer side than the riskier side of the mix but actually this is just an example of how tenuous standard return assumptions may be: many investors assume long-only government exposure will deliver excess returns of about 2.0% per annum because most government bond indices will yield that kind of return over the history they contain but, in fact, almost every major government bond index contains only a small part of available history, as they are calculated from 1981 or later.

Consequently, given that US treasury 10-year yields peaked in 1981 and declined steadily from that time until 2012, returns since then have looked impressive, but where they go from here depends largely on where yields are at the start of the sample period.

Taking a tactical view on top of broader diversification strategies may also yield excess returns, and this was particularly apposite during the debate about whether a major shift was occurring from bonds into equities.

According to pure RORO strategies the relatively recent performance of equities generally against bonds would have indicated a 'risk-on' environment overall, but again there are pockets of value within these general patterns wherein the real added-value lies.

In general, for most of the post-war period, rising bond yields have been inversely correlated with equity prices. When the technology bubble burst in 2000, the correlation reversed and became very closely correlated ever since the financial crisis: falling bond yields have been accompanied by falling equity prices as growth expectations collapsed.

However, the relationship between changes in bond yields and equity prices is different when the level of bond yields is very low compared with similar moves when the bond yield is higher: more specifically, there appeared for a long time to be an important inflection point around 4.5% yields or so: higher than this – when yields were more in line with long run averages – a rise in bond yields tended to be negative for equities and vice versa. Below this level, and in particular when yields fell to the very low levels that were experienced in recent years, the correlation tended to reverse; a fall in bond yields reflecting further declines in growth expectations that offset the benefit of a lower risk free rate. In effect, the lower risk free rate was more than offset by a higher required risk premium on equities, pushing their value down.

Playing The Central Bankers' Game

The challenge to these sorts of traditional assumptions means that a more intelligently calibrated approach to investment risk is the way forward, with solutions including identifying those strategies which are unaffected by RORO and/or modifying existing strategies to actively counter or exacerbate the RORO element. This includes dynamically hedging out its effects in a way that adapts to the changing strength of RORO and more perceptive portfolio construction.

This idea seems to have gained wider credence, given that the assets under management (AUM) of exchange traded funds (ETFs) that offer exposure to factors (e.g., value, growth), alternative benchmarks (e.g. volatility) or themes (e.g. momentum, carry) in the market not captured by traditional offerings have seen 166% growth in AUM since 2008, according to industry data.

This sort of diversification is not just at the usual sense of the asset class return level, but from additional diversification from strategies within asset classes (e.g. between carry in fixed income, which includes FX, and value in equities).

Indeed, before 2008 the markets could be termed either trend-friendly or carry friendly, but from then until 2012 they were neither one nor the other clearly and 2012 was bad for virtually all systems.

From that point markets seemed to have moved into an older market architecture where the central banks are acting in a way that does not interrupt the trends – be they in carry, momentum, or volatility – on a daily or intraday basis as they did in 2013.

Should markets revert to the ultra-intrusive central bank environment of 2012, then momentum trading done on a high frequency basis (as this capitalises well on short-term market microstructures) may prove again, as it did during that period, to be relatively impervious to the vagaries of the RORO environment.

Finding Value In Emerging Markets

The situation for emerging markets (EM) **requires a similarly nuanced approach, with RORO-delineated parameters according to the degree to which all assets correlate in a particular country or region, or whether they do so according to asset class, or any combination thereof, sometimes strongly manifesting themselves and sometimes not.**

The trick is to follow what's going on all the time across all key developed and emerging markets every day and to know inside and out what is happening on the fundamentals side of the countries involved.

In broad terms, of course, **all emerging markets can be regarded as the ultimate convergence trade,** in the same way that, for example, the valuations of eastern European countries in line for EU-accession gradually began to align (equities up, bond yields down, currencies strengthening) with those of EU countries the nearer to the accession they drew. How far off an EM is from having converged into being a DM, of course, can be seen from its credit rating, most palpably, aside from other tangential factors:

Moody's		S&P		Fitch		
Long-term	Short-term	Long-term	Short-term	Long-term	Short-term	
Aaa		AAA		AAA		Prime
Aa1		AA+	A-1+	AA+	F1+	High grade
Aa2	P-1	AA		AA		
Aa3		AA-		AA-		
A1		A+	A-1	A+	F1	Upper medium grade
A2		A		A		
A3	P-2	A-	A-2	A-	F2	
Baa1		BBB+		BBB+		
Baa2	P-3	BBB	A-3	BBB	F3	Lower medium grade
Baa3		BBB-		BBB-		
Ba1		BB+		BB+		Non-investment grade speculative
Ba2		BB		BB		
Ba3		BB-	B	BB-	B	
B1		B+		B+		Highly speculative
B2		B		B		
B3		B-		B-		
Caa1	Not prime	CCC+				Substantial risks
Caa2		CCC				Extremely speculative
Caa3		CCC-	C	CCC	C	In default with little prospect for recovery
Ca		CC				
		C				
C		D	/	DDD	/	In default
/				DD		

Consequently, **they could be regarded as pure 'risk-on' trades, whatever the asset class involved. However, within this encompassing description, there has been a re-emergence of those EMs that can be regarded as further along the development path than all of the others and thus investable in a marginally risk-off environment.**

Prior to 2008, the former group was probably best symbolised by the **BRIC** group, comprised of Brazil, Russia, India and China, which led the way on EM valuations by dint principally of their projected growth paths. These were followed by the **Next-11** (Mexico, Indonesia, South Korea, Turkey, Bangladesh, Egypt, Nigeria, Pakistan, the Philippines, Vietnam and Iran), of which the first four of the grouping had consistently outperformed the remainder, earning the sobriquet of the **'MIST'** countries along the way.

In pure currency trading terms, investment in selected emerging markets can accrue the benefits both of carry compensation in the short-term (which may or may not show up directly on your trading P&L sheets, depending on the platform you are using, but will be reflected in the movement of the currency overall) and of growth prospects supporting real exchange rate appreciation over the longer term.

The carry trade element of this is predicated, of course, upon the interplay of two key factors: wide (but stable) interest rate differentials (between the currency being sold to fund a higher-yielding currency) and low currency volatility on the first leg of the trade.

Before the 2008 crisis, the rolling correlation between returns from a traditional carry basket and returns from the S&P500 fluctuated around zero in developed markets and positive for emerging markets currencies. In the most recent major 'risk-on' environment, though, it is interesting to note that the same rolling correlation for both developed and emerging markets moved into positive territory.

Consequently, it might be said that either the emerging markets' currency carry trade risk has converged to that of the developed markets one or, more accurately, that this risk for developed markets' currencies has moved up the risk curve towards a level more associated with an EM currency equivalent. Indeed, holding a carry basket today is almost the equivalent of holding a pre-crisis carry basket together with some S&P futures. Given this more level playing field on the risk side of the equation, then, attention tends to focus on the underlying fundamentals of EM countries now and on their projections going forward.

In this regard, any gaps in the developed markets' landscape is likely to be filled increasingly over time by the currencies of those emerging economies that meet **the basic criteria of an investment destination:**

1. **A sustainable fiscal policy**
2. **A sound balance of payments profile**
3. **A solid financial and political system**

The **additional benefits of EM investment destinations is that more often than not they benefit both from momentum trading and carry trading strategies, given their relatively high interest rates in a broadly zero interest rate policy developed markets world.** In this context, it is highly likely that incrementally value-added returns will be accrued from investment in the BRICs, MIST and N-11 countries over time simply as they converge towards developed markets status.

Basic Convergence Premise

As mentioned above, in the most basic terms, **the reason for traders having become increasingly interested in emerging markets over the past decade in particular is the belief that, at some undefined point in the future, their fundamental characteristics will converge with those of the 'developed' markets (DM).**

Consequently, the idea runs, **there is money to be made as the risk involved in trading these EM assets declines, they are traded more and their assets gain in quality and return more true value.**

Indeed, as the relative risk perception between DM countries and EM ones began to narrow from around the 1980s investment flows into emerging markets increased from $25 billion in 1980 to $1.2 trillion in 2013, and over the past ten years alone these flows have averaged 5%-6% of GDP of the recipient countries, up from around 2% in the '80s and 4% in the '90s.

As a concrete example, all other things being equal, if the Indian rupee was regarded in precisely the same risk category as the US dollar, then the exchange rate between the two would go from the current level of around 60 rupees to the US dollar to just 1, parity: i.e. a 60:1 convergence.

The underlying notion of 'convergence' to developed market status underpins all emerging markets in general terms (including the even riskier 'frontier markets') but in recent years has been most obviously present in the currencies of countries that have been in various stages of joining the EU and then, it is logically inferred, the euro, although exactly the same process is relevant in trading terms to all other emerging markets at whatever stage of development they may be.

Euro Convergence Template

All of the countries that used to be part of the Soviet bloc but gained independence as the USSR disbanded saw their currencies gradually strengthen as the time of their accession to the euro grew closer. These were specifically entitled **'euro convergence trades'** and every one of them was an absolute winner.

For example, despite the appalling economic and then social consequences that have befallen Greece since its adoption of the euro in 2001, from the currency trading perspective it was a complete 'no-brainer' up to its accession. **Prior to joining the euro, there were, roughly, around 250 Greek drachma (GRD) to the US dollar. After it joined the euro project all drachma were replaced by euros, meaning that the rate had gone from 250 to under 1 within a year: nice trade indeed,** if you'd sold the drachma, and if you hadn't then clearly there was something profoundly wrong with you.

Exactly the same can be seen in the stock markets of those countries looking to join the EU. For example, Hungary's BUX stock exchange progress can be regarded for a long time as a simple convergence trade: first, away from the USSR and towards the West; secondly, from the West towards the EU; and thirdly, from the EU to the euro, as seen below:

Hungary BUX (15 Years, Monthly)

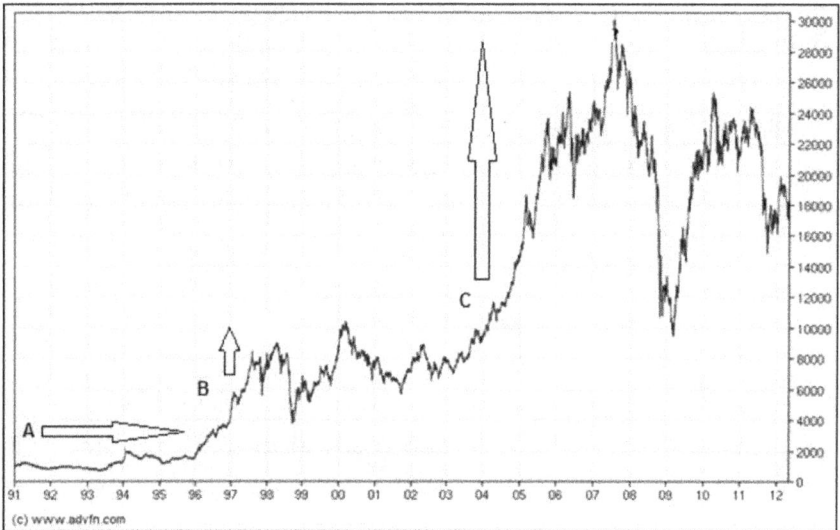

[Chart Key:

A = After the fall of the USSR in 1991, Hungary flatlines for a while before traders start to view it as gradually becoming an EU-grade state

B = Traders are regarding Hungary as an EU state more firmly by the month, as it approaches official EU accession date of 1 May 2004

C = Traders now looking for Hungary to replace the forint (HUF) with the euro at some point in the relatively near future]

Convergence-Driven Top-Down Trading Approach

In stock market terms, this approach is termed **'Top-Down Trading' but with a convergence twist (a positive paradigm shift).** This is an investment approach that involves looking at the big picture, beginning with the area in which a country is located, then the economic and political dimensions of that country including where it is in the business cycle, then the various sectors of the economy and then the specific details pertaining to a target company including management and key investment numbers and ratios.

A number of the greatest stock investors in history have used this style of trading to outperform all others in the market and we shall look at some of them as we proceed, but using George Soros and his partner Jim Rogers in their early days at Soros Fund Management is as good an example as any that I can think of.

The Rogers/Soros Classic Approach To Identifying Value In EM Trades

Basically, when they first began, whilst George was working through the numbers on his computer, Jim would be zooming around the world on his motorbike (later recalled in his book 'Investment Biker' – a very good read for those looking to invest in stocks in a top-down style, by the way) attempting to spot small changes at ground level in countries that were possibly on the cusp of major changes, through seeing tiny changes in general economic behaviour.

For example, typically this might involve Jim stopping off at a cafe in Hungary in the early 1990s and noticing that the locals were suddenly happy to spend a dollar (equivalent) on a cappuccino.

In Jim's mind this indicated the following rationale: people have more money to spend on small luxuries following Hungary's departure from the umbrella of the USSR in 1989 – therefore, people are earning more money as a whole – therefore, people are being paid more – therefore, companies are making more money – therefore, their earnings per share ratios will increase – therefore, current stock values will look cheap – therefore, domestic companies will attract more foreign investment – therefore, their corporate transparency will increase – therefore, their share price will continue to go up – therefore, more companies will float on the domestic stock exchange – therefore, more money will enter into the economy – and so on and so forth.

As one can see from the chart above, buying into a nation's changing broad economic architecture – in this case moving from the confines of the Soviet-style system to that of free enterprise and the increased consumerism that this entails – yielded exceptional results for Soros and Rogers.

This example can often be seen in areas that are undergoing such a shift in behavioural paradigm, as the same investment curve can be seen across the board, for example, in every country that broke away from the former Soviet Union (Poland, Czech Republic, Baltic States, etc etc).

In this respect, this investment story can be seen as the reverse of negative contagion.

In the case of the former Soviet Union itself exactly the same theory applied as well, although with a delayed effect to those of its former satellite states, as a break with centralised state control occurred only later on, under the presidency of Boris Yeltsin which began in December 1991.

Indeed, in the 'CE3 countries', the Polish stock market rose 150% in US dollar terms between 2000 and the end of 2005, Hungary by 179% and the Czech Republic by 338% (by contrast, the FTSE Eurofirst 300 index fell 5% in US dollar terms over the same time period).

Czech Republic and Poland Stock Exchanges (1999-2005)

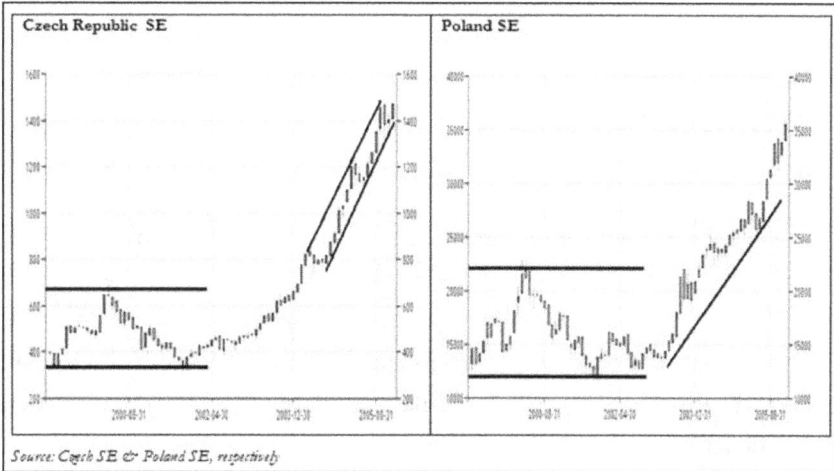

The returns – which were akin to shooting fish in a barrel – were even greater for the further outliers of eastern Europe, with Ukraine up 833% in US dollar terms over 2000-05, Romania up 757%, Slovakia up 607% and Estonia up 522%.

Ukraine and Romania Stock Exchanges (1999-2005)

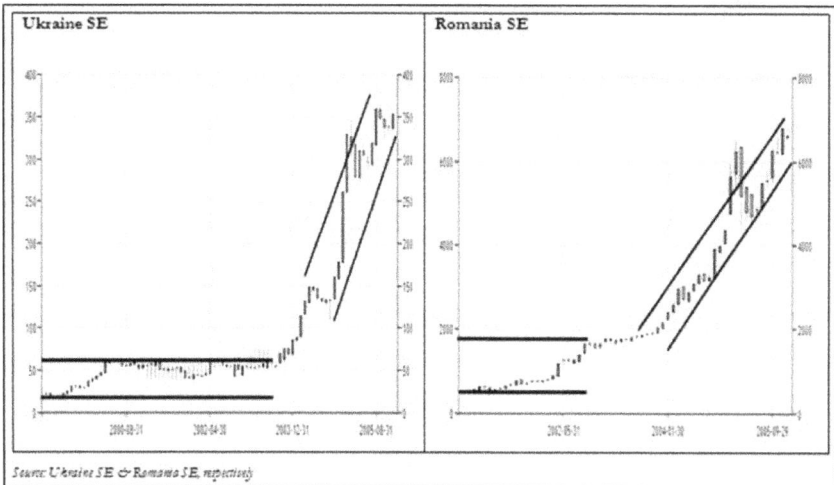

For those top-down investors who had learned the lesson from what happened to stocks (which are, after all, simply investment in companies, which are in turn an investment on the most basic level in a country's prosperity) in the former satellite nations of the USSR then the opportunity for the next phase of investment was obvious. This could be called a 'moving away from the Communist economic model' play colloquially.

One well-known fund manager, whom I cannot name as he is particularly fond of his and his fund's privacy, saw what had happened in the Former Soviet Union states and anticipated the same occurring in the newly formed Russian Federation after Yeltsin took power. Again the investment profile was identically bullish, as shown in the chart below.

Russian Stock Exchange (RTS) After Yeltsin Took Power

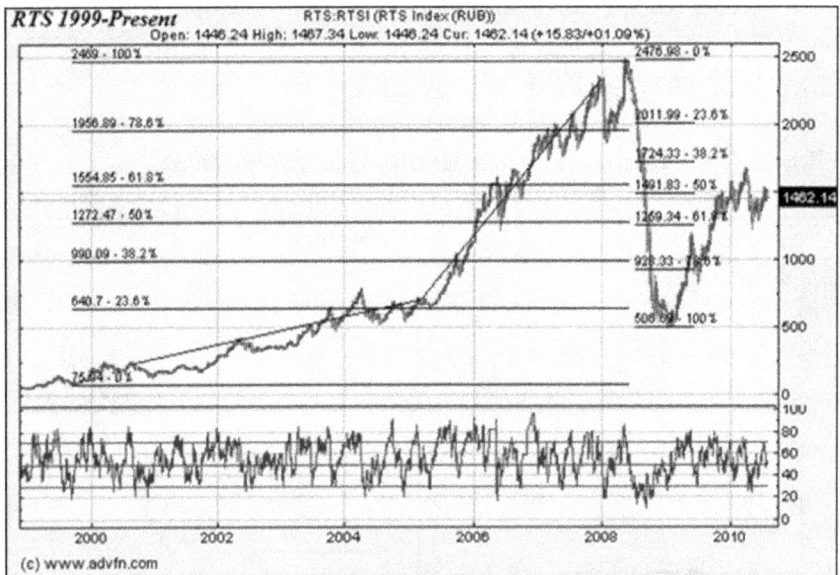

And this type of approach – of convergence from a 'less developed' (emerging) market to a more developed one – is

duplicated time and again across all markets and asset classes, and therein lie the real nuggets of value.

Still Plenty Of Value Left In Non-CEE Emerging Markets

This said, in broad terms, **the role of EM currencies as an internationally traded asset class is still remarkably limited compared to the increasing weight of their base economies in the global economic mix.**

As it stands, of the USD5.3trn daily turnover in the global FX markets, as determined by the Bank for International Settlements (BIS) 2013 Triennial Survey, at least 75% is still accounted for by the 'Big Four' international currencies: the US dollar (USD), the euro (EUR), sterling (GBP) and the Japanese yen (JPY).

In sharp contrast to this, the top three EM currencies totalled less than 7%, with the Mexican peso at 2.5% (vs. 1.3% in 2010), the Chinese renminbi at 2.2% (vs. 0.9%) and the Russian rouble at 1.6% (vs. 0.9%).

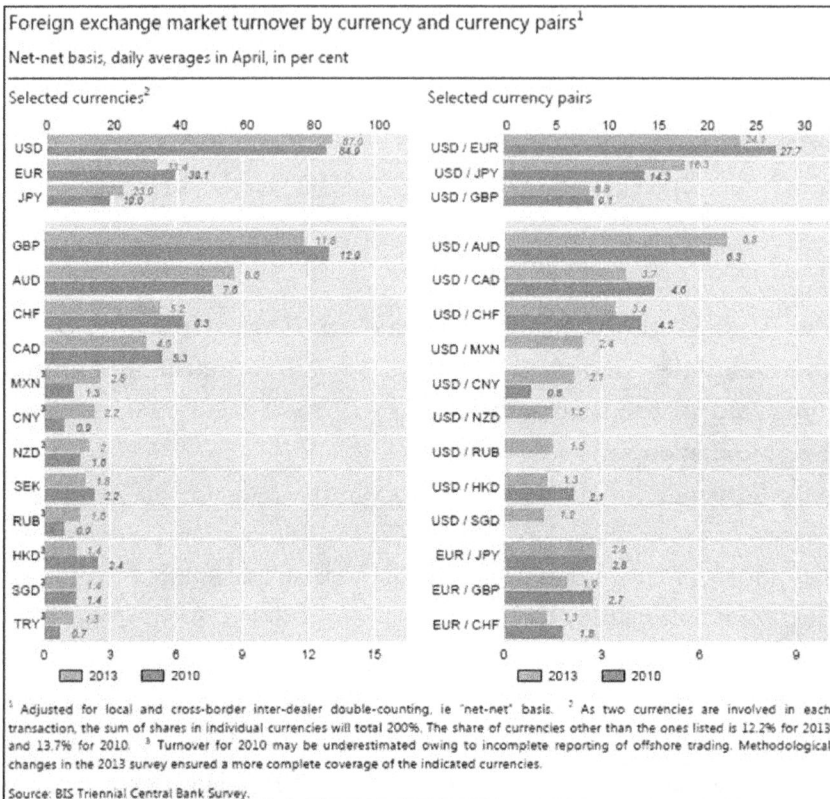

Foreign exchange market turnover by currency and currency pairs[1]

Net-net basis, daily averages in April, in per cent

[Chart showing "Selected currencies[2]" (left) and "Selected currency pairs" (right) with 2013 and 2010 data]

Selected currencies: USD 87.0/84.9, EUR 33.4/39.1, JPY 23.0/19.0, GBP 11.8/12.9, AUD 8.6/7.6, CHF 5.2/6.3, CAD 4.6/5.3, MXN 2.5/1.3, CNY 2.2/0.9, NZD 2/1.6, SEK 1.8/2.2, RUB 1.6/0.9, HKD 1.4/2.4, SGD 1.4/1.4, TRY 1.3/0.7

Selected currency pairs: USD/EUR 24.1/27.7, USD/JPY 18.3/14.3, USD/GBP 8.8/9.1, USD/AUD 6.8/6.3, USD/CAD 3.7/4.6, USD/CHF 3.4/4.2, USD/MXN 2.4, USD/CNY 2.1/0.8, USD/NZD 1.5, USD/RUB 1.5, USD/HKD 1.3/2.1, USD/SGD 1.2, EUR/JPY 2.8/2.8, EUR/GBP 1.9/2.7, EUR/CHF 1.3/1.8

[1] Adjusted for local and cross-border inter-dealer double-counting, ie "net-net" basis. [2] As two currencies are involved in each transaction, the sum of shares in individual currencies will total 200%. The share of currencies other than the ones listed is 12.2% for 2013 and 13.7% for 2010. [3] Turnover for 2010 may be underestimated owing to incomplete reporting of offshore trading. Methodological changes in the 2013 survey ensured a more complete coverage of the indicated currencies.

Source: BIS Triennial Central Bank Survey.

[Chart Key:
USD = US dollar/EUR= euro/JPY = Japan yen/AUD = Australia dollar/CHF = Switzerland franc/CAD = Canada dollar/MXN = Mexico peso/CNY = China yuan/NZD = New Zealand dollar/SEK = Sweden krone/RUB = Russia rouble/HKD = Hong Kong dollar/SG = Singapore dollar/TRY = Turkey lira]

Key Convergence Criteria

The explanation for this is that **in order to achieve a genuine leap into the big league of truly international currencies, EM currencies need:**

1. To have increasingly evident economic clout
2. To be used as an international reserve asset
3. To be utilised as a tool in invoicing and the settlement of international transactions
4. To be regarded as objects of speculative desire in FX volume trading (and therefore to possess FX regimes favourable to such free capital flows)

Increasing Economic Clout

In terms of economic growth and corollary trade flows alone, to begin with, **EM currencies should theoretically come to dominate the global FX landscape within a very short period.** By 2030, for example, the USD-valued economy of China will have overtaken that of the U.S. for the number one spot, according to various major finance houses, whose views are in line with those of the IMF.

By 2050, and maybe before, the Asian Tiger will have almost double the GDP of the States (in theory), with India ranked third, Brazil fourth, Mexico fifth, Russia sixth, Indonesia seventh; South Korea and Turkey will be thirteenth and fourteenth respectively. Indeed, already emerging market countries account for nearly half of global output, up from just over a quarter in 1971.

International Asset Usage

As we all know, **size is not everything, it is what you do with it that counts;** to put it less vernacularly, if you cannot trade it, it is not moving anywhere. **In some EM currency cases, stringent capital controls and fixed or highly managed FX regimes have led to a marked disconnect between trade flows and currency usage.**

In the case of the **long-vaunted BRICs** (Brazil, Russia, India, China), for example, although India and South Korea **notionally**

have free-floating exchange rates, in practice they are carefully managed by their central banks. In **Russia's case**, from 2000 to its financial crisis in 2008 a currency board system prevailed, with the rouble pegged to a basket (55% USD and the remainder EUR), with all changes in liquidity coming from the Central Bank of Russia's (CBR) sales and purchases of foreign currency.

This said, the recent signs are that the CBR has moved from FX rate targeting to inflation targeting and will not intervene aggressively unless the rouble looks like straying either side of a USDRUB band.

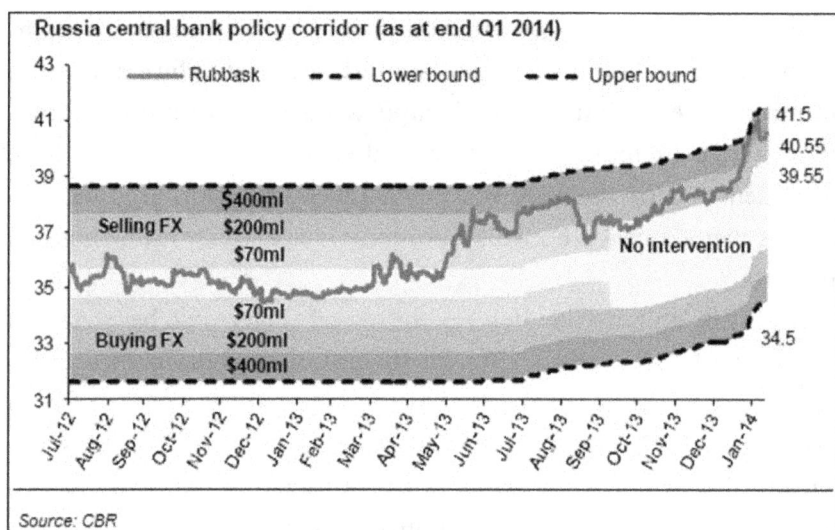

Russia central bank policy corridor (as at end Q1 2014)
Source: CBR

Additionally, during the height of the Ukraine crisis, the central bank policy allowed the currency a great degree of flexibility to float within a corridor against its target dollar-euro basket, and the central bank stated that it would set the amount of market interventions it took to shift the trading band on a daily basis, giving officials more flexibility in determining how many dollars it sold at a given price level before weakening the rouble's trading band. This was a major advantage for the rouble.

In **the case of China itself, the opportunity for any speculative gains remained highly limited for a very long period:** the central bank only widened the trading band for the RMB to 1% either side of a central rate of USDRMB6.8300 in April 2012, from the previous 0.5% variance, and then widened it out to a 2% variance in March 2014. There are major signs, though, as highlighted below, that **this situation is changing.**

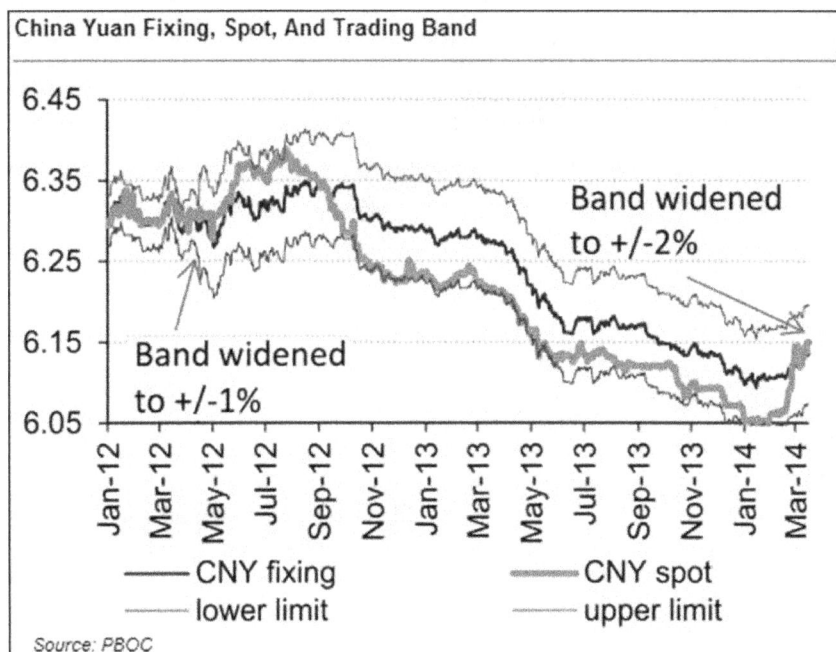

China Yuan Fixing, Spot, And Trading Band

Band widened to +/-2%

Band widened to +/-1%

CNY fixing   CNY spot
lower limit   upper limit

Source: PBOC

Usage In International Settlements and Transactions

Russia Template

In 2010 Russia's then First Deputy Prime Minister, Igor Shuvalov, said that a currency union between Russia, Belarus and Kazakhstan might be formed as a 'logical extension' to the introduction of the customs union between the three nations that came into effect on 1

January of that year. With an aggregated population of around 180mn people and accounting for about 83% of the GDP of the former USSR, the final hurdle for these three countries' planned formation of a single economic market by the end of 2012 would certainly be freedom of capital movement and the use of a common currency.

This idea was augmented by that of then Finance Minister, Alexei Kudrin, that the country was examining ways to sell its oil in roubles and that agreements in principle were struck in 2009 to allow trade between Russia, Belarus and China, to be conducted in roubles and Chinese renminbi.

A similar example of increasing use of a currency in international settlements and transactions has been seen in China as well recently, as part of a long-vaunted goal of allowing its currency to become fully convertible.

China Template

Renminbi trade settlement has taken off since a small pilot RMB trade settlement scheme was introduced in July 2009, to the extent that total trade settled in RMB increased four-fold in 2011 to reach RMB2.1trn (USD330bn), about 9% of China's total trade in that year. 2012 saw cross-border RMB trade settlement total RMB 2.94 trillion, about 12% of China's total trade.

Moreover, as early as November 2009 China had established RMB650bn in currency swaps to help importers in Argentina, Belarus, Hong Kong, Indonesia, Malaysia and South Kore, avoid having to pay in US dollars for Chinese goods (these **bilateral currency swaps now total around RMB2trn**), whilst recently it allowed all firms in the country to pay for imports and exports in RMB.

Whilst the RMB has been convertible under the current account for 15 years, recent steps have been taken to make it more convertible through the gradual liberalisation of the capital account, and **these moves to permit greater investment into real estate, stocks and bonds are set to gather in pace.**

Of course, China's capital account is partly open already, with **foreigners having full access to B shares but with A shares are restricted by strict quotas, whilst Chinese investors can buy foreign stocks via QDII funds but cannot make direct investments in overseas markets.** For a start, there is likely to be a further expansion of the QFII scheme that has opened China's domestic equity markets to overseas investors, which only recently saw the quota increase from USD30bn to USD80bn,and the RQFII (its RMB equivalent) from RMB20bn to RMB270bn.

A concomitant lifting of restrictions on foreign investors participating in the domestic bond market and the futures market, such as they are, is also widely expected, as is an increase in the quota for individual foreign exchange purchases, which currently stands at USD50,000 per year. As an adjunct to this, the pilot programme currently operating in Wenzhou – that permits domestic individuals to invest in overseas markets – is likely to be extended to other regions, and permission is likely to be given for foreign companies to raise RMB capital in onshore capital markets.

By 2011 there had been a boom in sales of China's non-financial bonds as well, which jumped to a record CNY200bn plus by the end of Q411, making the CNY the third most popular currency for corporate debt, behind the US dollar and the euro, and overtaking offerings in JPY for the first time ever. Such record bond issuance and looser regulations persuaded at least six overseas investment banks, including Goldman Sachs and UBS, to start underwriting local-currency debt.

In this regard, a key turning point was the announcement on 7 April 2010 that Standard Chartered's local China unit had become the first foreign-owned lender to trade Chinese corporate debt after a commercial-paper transaction. More recently in a similar vein, a landmark deal occurred in which UBS in London and HSBC Hong Kong branch carried out their first repurchase agreement in RMB by using Euroclear and the Hong Kong Monetary Authority to manage the collateral. This sort of repo-based deal would allow international financial institutions to use securities held with Euroclear as collateral to access liquidity from Hong Kong in RMB.

Building out the capital markets' temporal curve is also a prerequisite for RMB convertibility, and the keys to this will be more government and corporate bond issues across a range of maturities. Quite aside from anything else, this type of financing, rather than simply state-directed funding via the troubled state owned enterprise (SOE) vehicles, will produce the type of sustained and healthy high-quality efficient growth that the Chinese government now wants to replace the previous 'throw cash at everything' type of growth that traditionally creates asset price bubbles.

In this respect, throughout 2012 the China Banking Regulatory Commission (CBRC) asked banks to limit the size of loans to local government financing vehicles (LGFV) and enhance risk controls. With funding from banks capped, the LGFVs turned increasingly to the bond market and trusts to raise funds, so that during 2012 this new trust financing surged to RMB1.29trn from only RMB203bn in 2011, while new corporate bond financing increased from 1.366 trn in 2011 to 2.25 trn in 2012. Issuance of the LGFV bonds surged 148% in 2012 and accounted for some 50% of the net issuance of corporate bonds, and funds and wealth management products were the big buyers of these debts.

Once China has increased the use of the RMB as an investible asset, then the government's ultimate goal, of the currency being used significantly as a reserve currency, will become more attainable and will be of huge potential scope for retail traders. As long ago as the G20 summit in London in April 2010, Zhou Xiaochuan, Governor of the People's Bank of China

(PBOC) in Beijing, flagged the notion that the Chinese wanted a new global reserve currency to replace the US dollar at some point.

Initially, it was thought that Zhou simply wanted to expand the use of special drawing rights (SDRs), delineated as they currently are as a 95% mix of the four key currencies of USD, EUR, GBP and JPY, but in later conversations it appeared **that the Chinese thought that incorporating an element of the RMB into the mix and using the newly redrawn SDR (including the RMB constituent) would be the best way of proceeding in this regard.** In practical terms, as the SDR is currently used, the renminbi being in the mix is not that important from the perspective of trading volumes, but for the Chinese authorities it is a very important symbol of the country's standing on the world stage. **Indeed, many think that the renminbi will be included in the SDR mix before 2015.**

Fundamentals Remain Key
To Finding Value In EM

Asia

In all of these cases again, though, as is often exemplified in emerging markets trading, fundamental considerations are key, and for Asia much of this hinges on the outlook for China.

That said, China has a massive problem with its rising and massive debt burden, especially for the state-owned enterprise sector (SOE). Essentially the problem has been that in order to stimulate the type of 10% plus growth in GDP per year that was seen in China over the past decade or so, the government directed local governments to hand out money for projects like it was going out of fashion.

This had three key effects: first, a lot of it went 'missing' in the pockets of officials who then spent it on buying up property (causing the bubble-type scenario that we now see in the country), second, the same officials and local dignitaries then poured money into the domestic stock exchange (hence the inexorable rise for a while of the Shanghai Composite) and third, it has left virtually every sizeable business (including banks, trusts, finance houses, construction firms and so on and so on) with massive amounts of debt on their books.

Shanghai Composite SE (10 Years, Monthly)

[Chart Key:

A = Money makes its way from the CNY4 trillion (USD586 million) 2008/09 economic stimulus package into the domestic stock market, following a major collapse from the 6,000 level as the global financial crisis took hold in 2007/08

B = Concerns over rising debt levels of SOEs (see elsewhere) increase markedly, capping gains at around the 3,500 level

C = Range established of 1,700-3,500]

Consequently **any rise in interest rates could cause a major default, which would have a ripple effect of causing more defaults. The danger is that this could then lead to an economic implosion that would be felt around the globe**, given that China is the world's biggest importer of a lot of stuff, particularly raw materials.

And this, aside from the correlations between EM and DM markets that occur on a daily, ongoing basis, is why the retail trader needs now only to watch the big data releases from the G10 or G2-developed countries, but also, crucially, needs to watch the data that comes out of China.

In this regard, the key numbers to look out for are the Purchasing Managers Indices, especially for manufacturing (which indicates how much stuff China is likely to buy from the rest of the world going forward): this ranges from 0 to 100, with any number below 50 indicating a contraction and any number above 50 indicating an expansion.

Returning to my point about how the outlook for China has a huge effect on markets such as commodities and commodity-related currencies, not to mention all of Asia (stock markets and currencies), and feeds into the asset markets of many other EM countries, below we can see the effect of a very disappointing manufacturing PMI release (of April's numbers) on 5 May 2014 on a few selected assets.

China Manufacturing PMI Performance (1 Year)

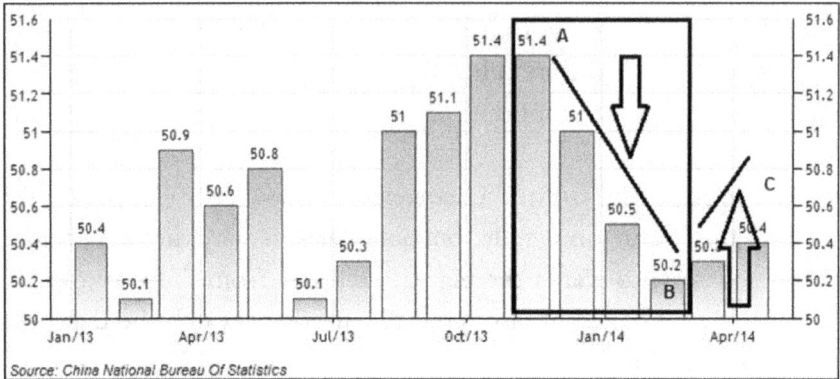

Source: China National Bureau Of Statistics

[Chart Key:
PMI = 0 to 100 index, with any reading of under 50 indicating an economic contraction and any over 50 indicating an economic expansion over the sample period; however, any downturn shows a decline in directional momentum, of course]

The AUD, to kick off with, would have been the obvious starting point to capitalise on the vicissitudes of China's PMI, given that China over the past decade or so has accounted for around 30% of Australia's total exports; indeed, this was not lost on the markets, as shown below.

AUDUSD (1 Year, Daily)

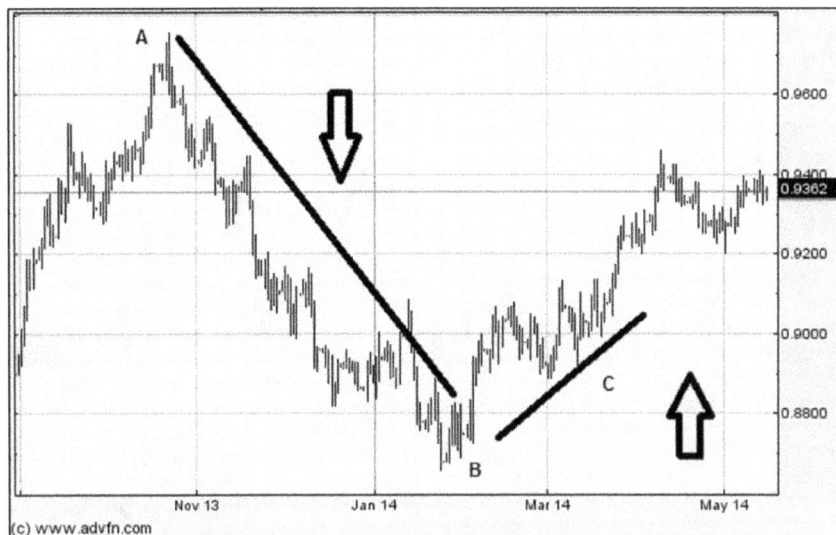

[Chart Key:

A = *Negative reversal of China PMI trend, AUD begins weakening trend*

B = *Bottom of weakening China PMI trend, AUD starts to strengthen*

C = *As China PMI gains ground, so does the AUD]*

Simply following the first downpath of China's PMI – without then following it back up – would have yielded the following trade:

1. Sell AUD, GBP10 per point at 0.9735 resistance level, stop loss at next resistance at 0.9790
2. Buy back at support level of 0.8930
3. **Total Profit = GBP8,050 on a risk/return ratio of nearly 16X**

Many platforms now quote copper or, failing that, ETFs; copper was a key beneficiary of China's construction-led boom, as in an average US house enough copper is used to fill an Olympic-sized swimming pool. I will not go into the trade here for the simple reason that it is sometimes quoted in pounds or ounces or other individual ways, so is less than universal in application.

Copper (1 Year, Daily)

[Chart Key:
A = Negative reversal of China PMI trend, copper begins weakening trend
B = Bottom of weakening China PMI trend, copper starts to strengthen
C = As China PMI gains ground, so does copper]

Japan has been a key beneficiary as well of China's economic expansion over the past 10 years and is also linked in the minds of investors to China's fortunes simply by dint of its geographic proximity.

Japan Nikkei 225 Stock Index (1 Year, Daily)

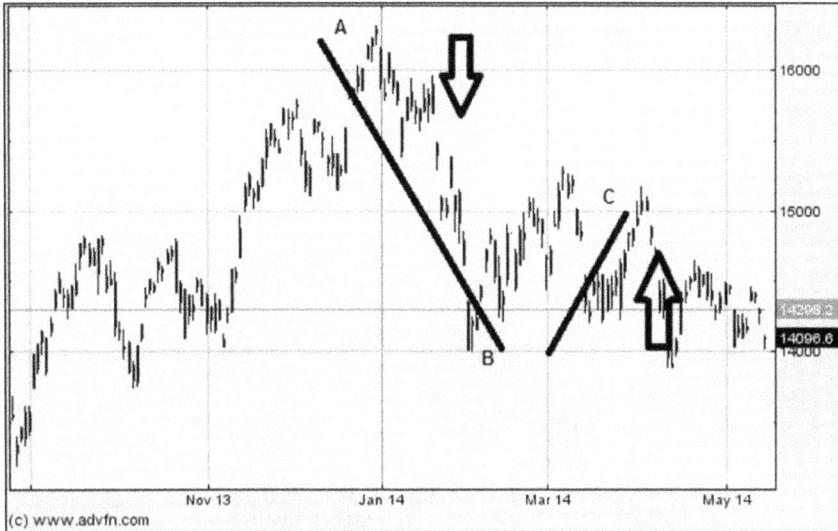

[Chart Key:
A = Negative reversal of China PMI trend, Nikkei begins weakening tend
B = Bottom of weakening China PMI trend, Nikkei starts to strengthen
C = As China PMI gains ground, so does the Nikkei, until domestic factors
stall further gains]

So, again, simply following the first downpath of China's PMI –
without then following it back up – would have yielded the following
trade:

1. Sell Nikkei, GBP10 per point at the key 16,000 level, stop loss
   at next resistance at 16,100
2. Buy back at support level of 14,100
3. **Total Profit = GBP19,000 on a risk/return ratio of nearly
   20X**

**Conversely, and following exactly the same trends and timings,
the traditional safe-haven for rising global risk – the CHF –**

performs in exactly that function, according to the direction of China's PMI: that is, when China's PMI starts to fall, the CHF strengthens (as below, against the USD); when China's PMI bottoms out, so does the CHF; and when China's PMI starts to recover, the CHF begins to weaken.

USDCHF (1 Year, Daily)

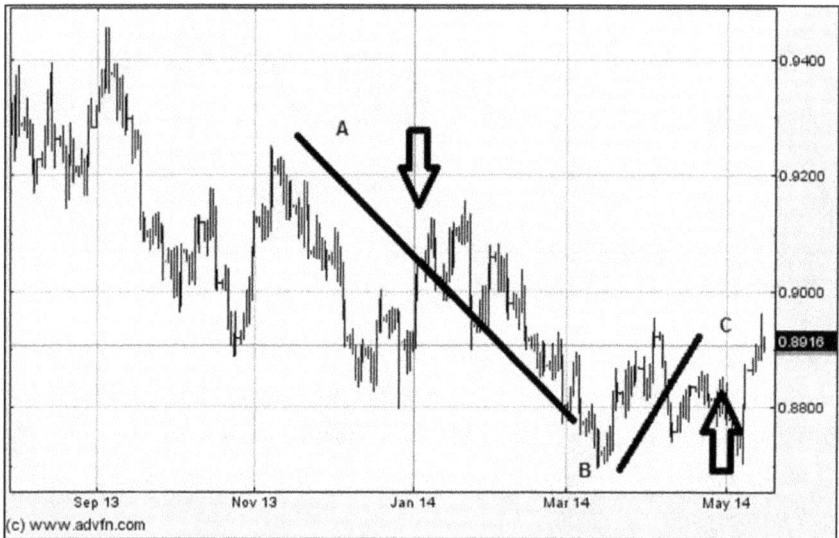

[Chart Key:
A = CHF strengthens against the USD, as China PMI weakens
B = CHF bottoms out against the USD, as China PMI flattens out
C = CHF weakens against the USD, as China PMI strengthens]

The trade, then – of inversely tracking China's PMI with the CHF (or directly tracking it with the USD, if you prefer to see it that way) – would be:

1. Sell CHF, buy USD, GBP10 per point at the key 0.9245 resistance level, stop loss at next resistance at 0.9295
2. Buy back at support level of 0.8690

3. Total Profit = GBP5550 on a risk/return ratio of over 10X

Latin America

One of the most interesting dynamics observed in the emerging FX (EMFX) markets since the beginning of 2014 has been the broad resilience of Latin American (LatAm) asset prices to recent global shocks, notably including fears over China's growth slowdown, as so many of the region's economies have been particular beneficiaries in the past of China's golden growth years.

In broad terms, it could be said that the two countries' currencies that had the greatest exposure to China's uber-growth – the Chilean peso (CLP) and the Venezuelan bolivar (VEB) – are set to do worse in the coming few months and years as China's growth settles at a lower rate and changes in nature from a manufacturing-fuelled one to a consumer-led one, whilst that with the least exposure – the Mexican peso (MXN) – should be an outperformer (see chart below).

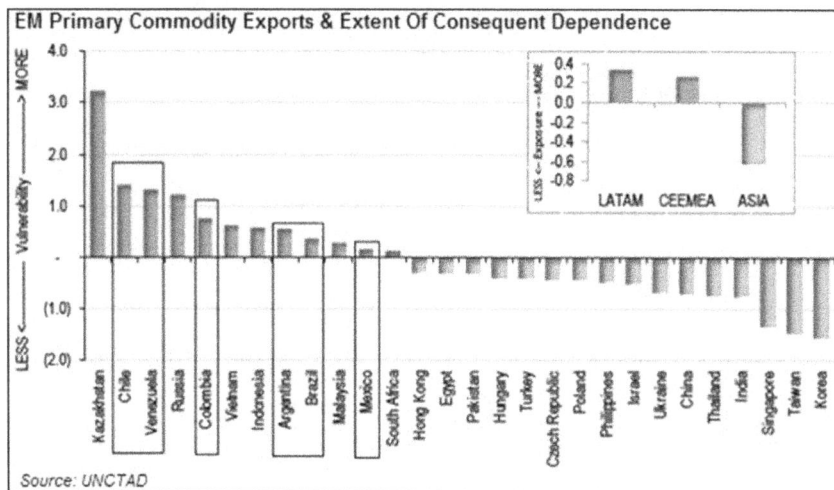

EM Primary Commodity Exports & Extent Of Consequent Dependence

Source: UNCTAD

However, despite being the third most exposed to the China-dominated commodities sector, **the LatAm FX sector should not** be regarded as likely to move as one risk-on/risk-off asset class, dependent on any external factors, but because the degree of investor involvement has been low, LatAm FX still offers a risk-reward profile driven by individual stories that minimise global exposure and provide very clean positioning.

In broad terms, while LatAm FX was appreciating, the main concern of FX policies across the region was growth and thus the bias to intervene to weaken currencies, but the coin flipped at the beginning of 2014; with LatAm FX now on a multi-year depreciation trend, sooner or later the focus of FX policy will shift to preventing pass-through pressures onto inflation.

In Brazil and Peru this process began in Q1 2014, with both central banks engaged in sizable and consistent USD selling programs. In Brazil's case, the inflation dimension remained a particularly sensitive subject, given the country's history of hyperinflation, and with presidential elections scheduled for October 2014 and tradable goods inflation in annual terms having doubled by the beginning of Q2 2014 from 3% to around 6% since 3Q12 (tracking the depreciation of the BRL) the authorities remained very wary of additional pressures coming via a weaker real.

USDBRL (1 Year, Daily)

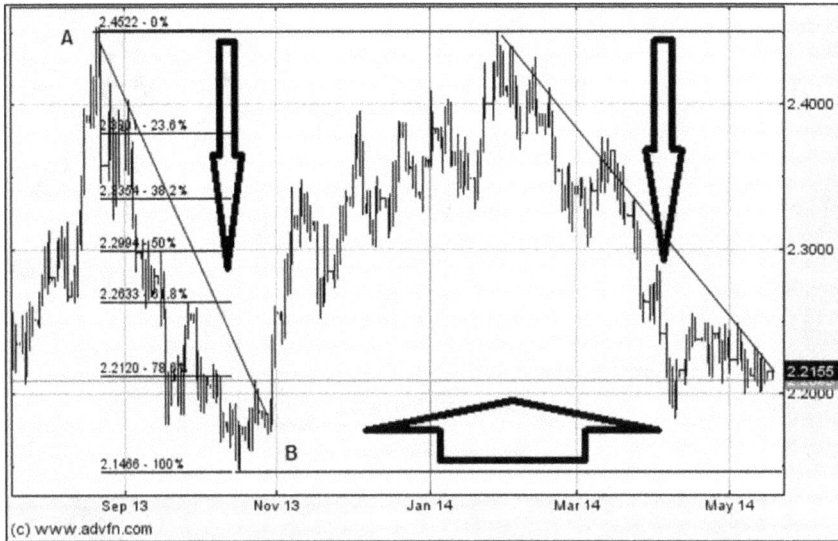

[Chart Key:

A = Central Bank of Brazil tasked with keeping inflationary pressures under control by selling USD and buying BRL @2.45

B = Fundamental pressure and speculative buying of USDBRL acts as a floor]

In **Peru, the impact of a weaker PEN on tradable and imported goods has been even more pronounced,** with annual core inflation running at around 3.8% over the first half of 2014 and imported goods inflation having shot up from 0% to 4.8% in less than a year.

Indeed, the Central Bank of Peru (BCRP) acknowledged early in 2014 that "inflation is forecast to remain initially close to the upper band of the target due to the lagging effect of the supply shocks" before converging back towards the 2% mid-point target, and all of this whilst growth is decelerating.

USDPEN (6 Months, Daily)

[Chart Key:
A = Central Bank of Peru tasked with keeping inflationary pressures under control by selling USD and buying PEN, all the way down from 2.8245
B = Fundamental pressure and speculative buying of USDPEN acts as a floor]

Despite the hawkish comments about the US's rates trajectory from the Yellen testimony in the first half of 2014 for the following months, **Mexico's fundamentals, notably its inflation numbers and growth, look appealing for the foreseeable future,** all other things remaining equal. In addition, Mexico is one of the very few countries to have issued a 100-year USD1bn (2110) sovereign bond, which was priced to yield a very competitive 5.96% – a palpable endorsement from the international investment community as to its 'converging' potential.

With growth in the world's largest copper producer – Chile – likely to continue to slow, as demand from China's construction sector continues to diminish (the average US house uses enough copper in pipes to fill an Olympic-sized swimming pool), being long MXNCLP for the foreseeable future looks like a sound idea, despite **Chilean Finance Minister Felipe Larrain's view that the country is on track to achieve developed-nation status ahead of the 2018 target.**

At the other end of the spectrum for most market players remains the Argentine peso, with Argentina the most extreme example in the region of the depletion of FX reserves resulting from unwillingness to allow a free float of the currency.

Indeed, through a combination of official appropriation of reserves for the payment of USD liabilities and active intervention via USD sales, reserves fell from a peak of USD52.5bn at the beginning of 2011 to below USD30bn by the end of Q1 2014.

It is interest that the **Colombian peso fared especially well at the end of Q1 2014 specifically on the news that JPMorgan Chase increased the weight of Colombia in its local-currency bond indices, the GBI-EM Global Diversified and GBI-EM Global.** It is extremely important for retail traders to notice when this happens.

This sort of re-weighting – this is not a credit ratings issue, by the way – can materially impact an asset, as it means that major real money funds (pension funds etc) can concomitantly increase their holdings of an asset in their overall investment portfolios, and that means a lot more potential money flowing into it.

USDCOP (1 Year, Daily)

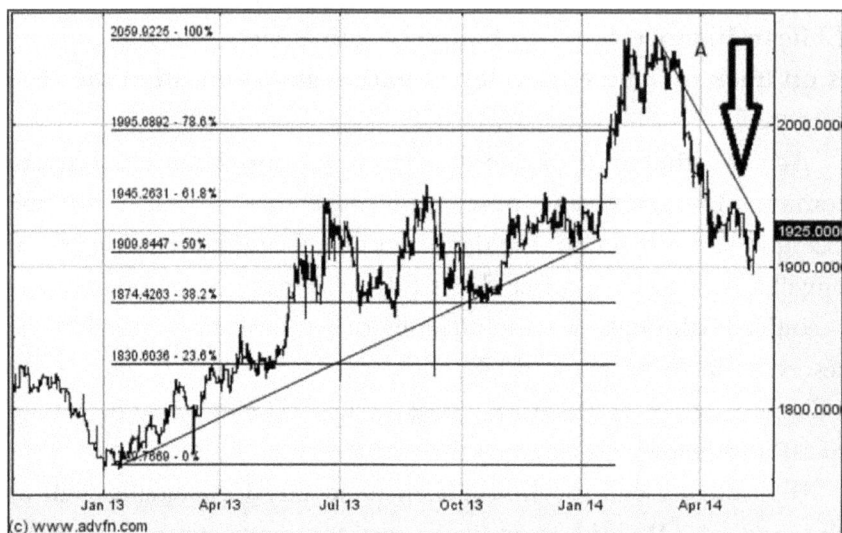

[Chart Key:
A = Huge strengthening of the COP against the USD on the basis alone of the
JPMorgan re-weighting in key indices]

In the case of Colombia, the peso appreciated markedly, with expectations that its weight in the GBI-EM Global Diversified was likely to increase to 8.0% from 3.2%, and to 5.6% from 1.8% in the GBI-EM Global, with a broader range of bonds also included in a phased approach over five month-end periods starting on 30 May and ending on 30 September 2014: indeed, it is estimated that the re-weighting translated into around $9.4bn of additional demand for these bonds (and thus the currency) within the preceding month or so of the actual re-weighting.

Moreover, quite aside from the initial market reaction to the announcement, the potential for further benefits for Colombia's local bonds and currency in the following months was evident as, for a start, the balance of payments impact of such an inflow was significant.

As an adjunct to this, the greater demand for Colombian debt was regarded as being helpful for the government to lower its funding costs and diversifying the country's investor base away from only local players (at the time of the re-weighting announcement, just over 6% of local bonds were held by non-residents in Colombia, while in countries like Brazil, Mexico and Peru these levels bordered 17%, 35% and 50% respectively), and it was estimated that this ratio for Colombia could reach around 17% if the full amount of possible inflows materialised.

Having said all of this, the fact remains that the actual number of countries that have successfully made the transition from emerging markets to developed markets is remarkably limited. **According to a study by Standard Life Investments in Edinburgh, just five of the 38 countries with stock markets in 1900 have moved from emerging to developed market status as of now.** Of the rest, 17 were and are developed, 14 were and are classified as middle-income emerging. In fact, those with developed markets in 1900 still dominate the equity landscape, comprising 84% of the MSCI All World Index.

Nonetheless, as mentioned often before, **the truth does not actually matter that much in investment terms: it's the perception of reality that counts.**

Long-Term Global Economic Cycles

As I mentioned at the very start of this book, and as I think I have already often illustrated, **markets are subject to the manifestation of a wide variety of patterns; the key to trading success is identifying what they are and how to extract the optimal value from them.**

In the simplest of terms, they can be looked at in terms of duration: there are short-term patterns that mostly relate to technical analysis and there are longer-term ones that generally relate to broad economic factors (such as interest rates, inflation, GDP growth and so forth).

However, even beyond these, **there are broad-based long-term cycles** that relate to all of the above: **in technical analysis terms, for example, the Elliot Wave** (as described in the *Technical Analysis section on page 137*) is a good example; and in **economic terms the convergence of an economy** from 'frontier' market status to 'emerging' and then to 'developed' is another.

In this latter regard, though, there are significant consequences for trading – particularly for the interest rates and volatility components thereof – that the trader has to know about, in order to make sense of the underlying trend against which they are trading, be it in FX, bonds (which, as I have mentioned before, is basically FX by another name), commodities, or stocks.

The Kondratieff Wave

In global terms (we will get to the specifics for regions and asset classes in a moment) to kick off with, the trader needs to be aware of the Kondratieff Wave ('K-Wave') – named after a Russian economist active in the 1920s named Nikolai Kondratieff – which seeks to show that **there are long-term cycles in the entire global capitalist economy of between 45 and 60 years – and even much longer – each that are self-correcting and evolving and are defined by the emergence of new industries in ongoing technological revolutions.** As an adjunct of this, each major cycle involves the destruction of much of the past cycle and the concomitant evolution of new innovation.

Kondratieff's theory has been refined/distorted – however you want to look at it – by various people since, but the consensus of the major examples over the past few hundred years would be: the 1770s' Industrial Revolution, the 1820s' Steam and Railways age beginning, the 1870s' Steel and Heavy Engineering move, the 1900s' era of Oil, Electricity, Automobiles and Mass Production and the 1970s' shift to the age of Information and Telecommunications.

It is interesting to note at this point that – arguably, although not much – the world's most successful stock investor ever, Warren Buffett, bases his investment strategy on such fundamental paradigmatic shifts; seeking to identify the onset of a new cycle (or 'wave'), buying shares in as many solid new cycle-related businesses as he can and just sitting on them.

It is also interesting to note, as we touched on Elliot Waves just a moment earlier, that we could regard the nature of these cycles in Elliot Waves' terms.

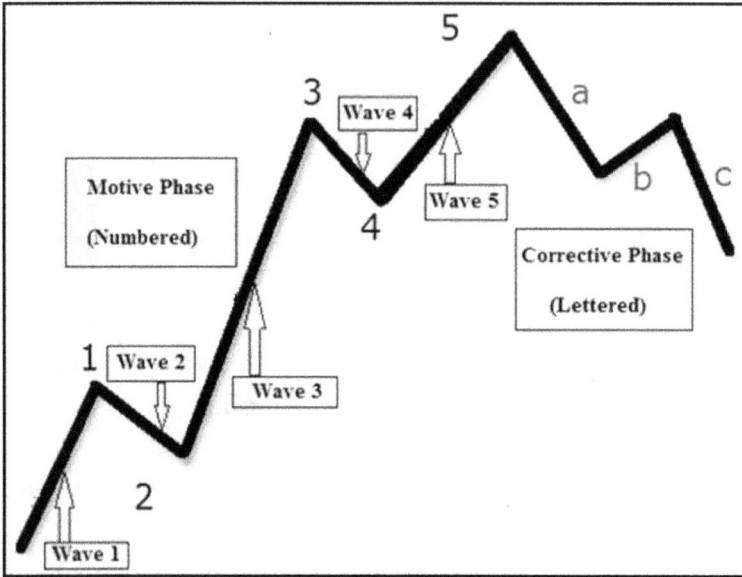

That is, that at the onset of a long-term economic cycle there is likely to be a lack of confidence and a fear of falling back into slump or depression, before inflation, interest rates and credit slowly start to rise as confidence in the new age increases (you might say, Elliot Wave 1).

As the economy expands (indicated in this instance by inflation) and interest rates increase as an adjunct to this, then so business and consumer confidence grows further and credit is extended more (Elliot Wave 3 correlation).

As we enter into the final up-phase of the move, confidence levels morph into over-exuberance and extraordinary loose 'bubble-like' credit conditions, with interest rates also declining (Elliot Wave 5 correlation).

Finally, rising concerns over loose credit, inflationary upward spiral and bad debt causes business and consumer reticence to embark on new projects (in business terms, expansion, and in consumer terms, new purchases), default rates increase, credit is squeezed, the economic outlook turns negative, unemployment rises, disinflation turns into deflation and we have a negative world view.

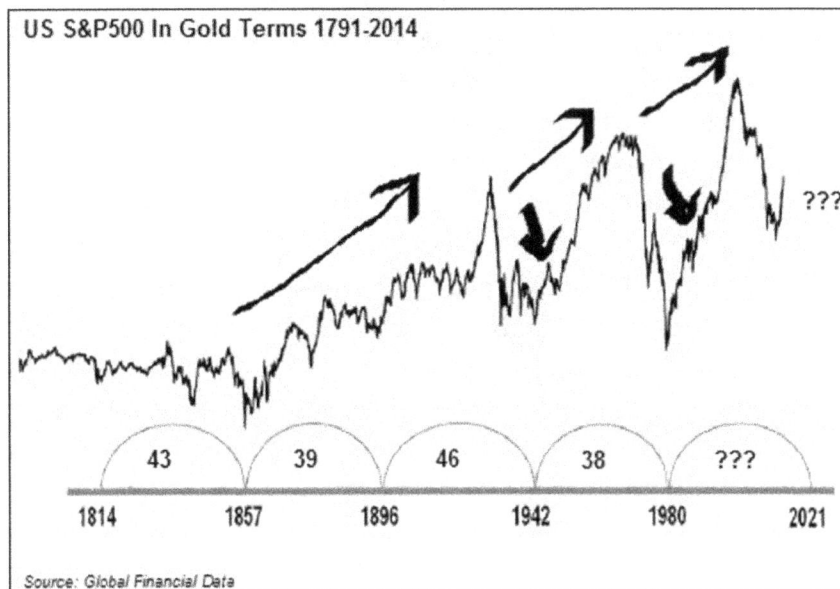

US S&P500 In Gold Terms 1791-2014

43	39	46	38	???
1814	1857	1896	1942	1980	2021

Source: Global Financial Data

Consequently, it would be fair to say that based on this time set the **US stock market, and for that matter the UK one and those of the major northern European countries, are currently in an overall cyclical downturn and that, for the time being, the overall trend – economically and in terms of asset prices, interest rates and volatility – will be net down over the next few years.**

The Business Cycle

Within this, though, there other shorter-time patterns manifesting themselves in the classic business cycle, which is the recurring level of business activity that changes in an economy over a period of time. The four stages of a cycle (although some maintain that there are five) are: full scale recession, early recovery, late recovery and early recession.

Since the Second World War, most business cycles have lasted between three to five years from peak to peak, with the average duration of an expansion being nearly four years and the average length of a recession being just under a year, although as we have seen in the most recent recession (and in the Great Depression era) recessions can last a lot longer.

According to the USA's National Bureau of Economic Research (NBER), the US has experienced 12 recessions (including the most recent one) and 11 expansions since the end of the Second World War.

US Business Cycles Since 1857 (NBER)

BUSINESS CYCLE REFERENCE DATES		DURATION IN MONTHS			
Peak	Trough	Contraction	Expansion	Cycle	
Quarterly dates are in parentheses		Peak to Trough	Previous trough to this peak	Trough from Previous Trough	Peak from Previous Peak
	December 1854 (IV)	--	--	--	--
June 1857(II)	December 1858 (IV)	18	30	48	--
October 1860(III)	June 1861 (III)	8	22	30	40
April 1865(I)	December 1867 (I)	32	46	78	54
June 1869(II)	December 1870 (IV)	18	18	36	50
October 1873(III)	March 1879 (I)	65	34	99	52
March 1882(I)	May 1885 (II)	38	36	74	101
March 1887(II)	April 1888 (I)	13	22	35	60
July 1890(III)	May 1891 (II)	10	27	37	40
January 1893(I)	June 1894 (II)	17	20	37	30
December 1895(IV)	June 1897 (II)	18	18	36	35
June 1899(III)	December 1900 (IV)	18	24	42	42
September 1902(IV)	August 1904 (III)	23	21	44	39
May 1907(II)	June 1908 (II)	13	33	46	56
January 1910(I)	January 1912 (IV)	24	19	43	32
January 1913(I)	December 1914 (IV)	23	12	35	36
August 1918(III)	March 1919 (I)	7	44	51	67
January 1920(I)	July 1921 (III)	18	10	28	17
May 1923(II)	July 1924 (III)	14	22	36	40
October 1926(III)	November 1927 (IV)	13	27	40	41
August 1929(III)	March 1933 (I)	43	21	64	34
May 1937(II)	June 1938 (II)	13	50	63	93
February 1945(I)	October 1945 (IV)	8	80	88	93
November 1948(IV)	October 1949 (IV)	11	37	48	45
July 1953(II)	May 1954 (II)	10	45	55	56
August 1957(III)	April 1958 (II)	8	39	47	49
April 1960(II)	February 1961 (I)	10	24	34	32
December 1969(IV)	November 1970 (IV)	11	106	117	116
November 1973(IV)	March 1975 (I)	16	36	52	47
January 1980(I)	July 1980 (III)	6	58	64	74
July 1981(III)	November 1982 (IV)	16	12	28	18
July 1990(III)	March 1991(I)	8	92	100	108
March 2001(I)	November 2001 (IV)	8	120	128	128
December 2007 (IV)	June 2009 (II)	18	73	91	81
Average, all cycles:					
1854-2009 (33 cycles)		17.5	38.7	56.2	56.4*
1854-1919 (16 cycles)		21.6	26.6	48.2	48.9**
1919-1945 (6 cycles)		18.2	35.0	53.2	53.0
1945-2009 (11 cycles)		11.1	58.4	69.5	68.5

* 32 cycles
** 15 cycles

Source: NBER

Having said that, as mentioned earlier – particularly in the section looking at emerging markets – **different regions and countries within regions are not all at the same point of their overall business cycle, despite their being part of the long-running K Waves** that are a part of their being in the global economy.

Emerging Asia And Latin America

China aside, as although in strict Elliot Wave terms it looks to be on an upward wave there are many more basic questions over the sustainability of its debt profile as discussed earlier, **emerging Asia has many markets that are in a long-term secular bull run, with the standout ones currently being Taiwan and Vietnam,** although there are compelling arguments for many others (Philippines, Malaysia and Indonesia, and eventually India and Thailand).

In Taiwan, for example, following the almost two decade-long triangle wave IV, it appears to be increasingly evident that the cycle degree wave V is in operation, which means that, as long as 7685 holds as support on the TAIEX index the structure will stay bullish. For Vietnam, in the meantime, the Ho Chi Minh Stock index is subdividing in a powerful cycle degree wave III, with major support around the 490 level.

In Latin America, the **Brazilian stock market** has been underperforming global stock market indices since 2010 but now the price action is producing evidence that a new bull market is beginning. As long as the 2013 low of 44,107 remains in place the technical structure would point to the cessation of the long period of consolidation from the 2010 high and indicate that a third wave higher should be underway; well above the all-time (2008) high of 73,920.

Brazil Bovespa (12 Years, Monthly)

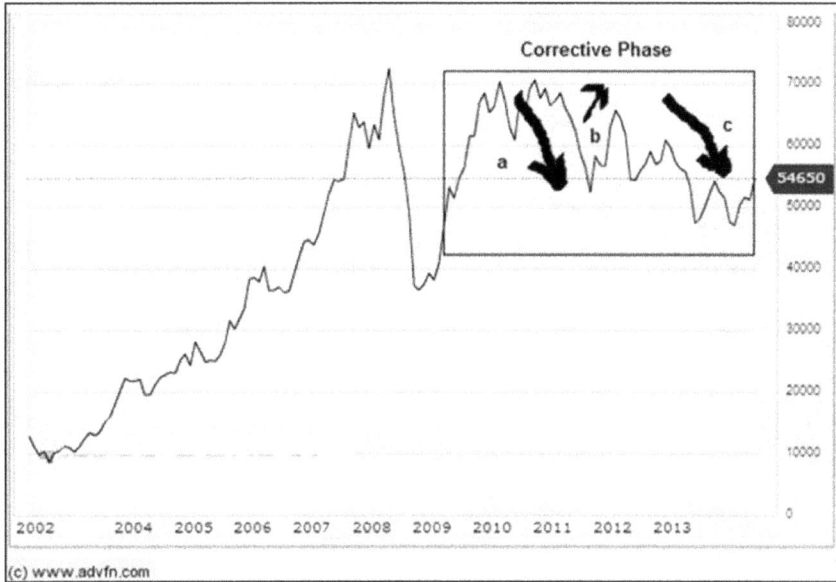

[Chart Key:
Please see 'Elliot Waves' earlier]

Additionally, and given more fuel by its much better overall economic and political profile (see earlier), the **Mexican stock market** looks like the a-b-c Elliot Wave Correctional Move lower from the January 2013 high has been completed and that a new Motive Phase upwards may be beginning.

Mexico IPC (5 Years, Weekly)

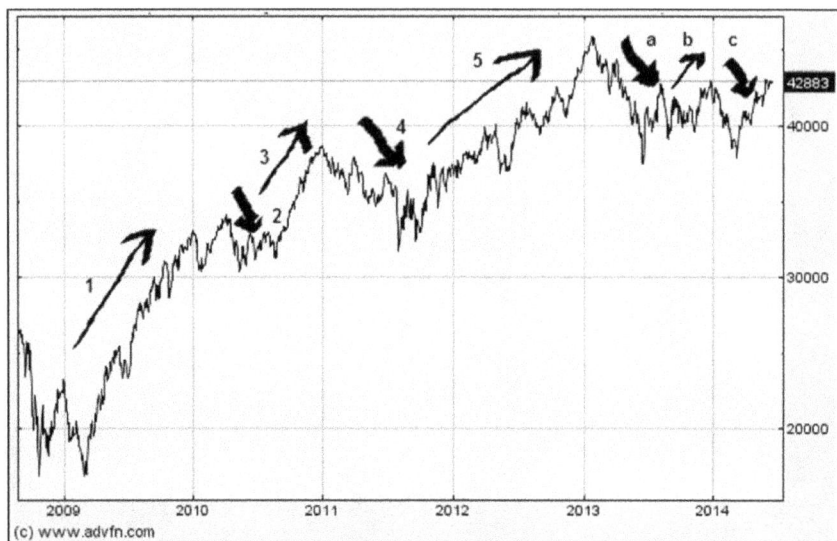

[Chart Key:
Please see 'Elliot Waves' earlier]

Commodities

The basic problem trading commodities – as I touched on in the first section of this book – is either: ongoing, huge manipulation, principally by the world's major central banks (in the case of gold mainly, but also silver); or the slowdown in the growth prospects of China (for the base metals that are most used in infrastructure expansion, most notably, perhaps, copper).

For a long time as we know in this latter regard, base metals were caught in a metals super-cycle of bull prices, whilst the precious metals also traded higher overall principally as hedges against inflation and the PGMs stayed buoyant due to their use in industry (catalytic converters being the obvious example).

Looking at these from a long-term technical basis, though, is instructive: **the US dollar price of gold topped out in September 2011 as bullish sentiment peaked and, with the ongoing manipulation a test of a low around the USD1,000/Oz mark looks possible. However, gold also maintains a bullish long-term wave structure versus the fiat currencies (USDJPY is a good example of this). Gold only had a brief period above its 1980 high versus European currencies and the subsequent reversal lower is the biggest factor stacking up against the gold bull case.**

Coming back to where we started – on volatility – and in common with other macro markets the volatility (as measured by monthly Bollinger Band Width) of all commodities remains extremely low: it is at a four-decade low in Brent Crude Oil and at an all-time low in the S&P GSCI Commodity Index.

Overall, then, judging from the long-term charts, gold should be a buy, together with silver, but, until the regulatory authorities get around to dealing with the manipulation of the gold market (this may be some time, given they may be dealing with FX and oil market manipulation for some time to come) it is probably wise to stay out of it and look to buy gold when technicals and fundamentals become ludicrously low (i.e. anywhere around the USD1,000/Oz mark).

The Minsky Cycle

I did say that most things, aside from the machinations of God, move according to patterns. The 'Minsky Cycle' is another important element in the understanding of where one is in the overall global investment mix (which means, in practical terms, narrowing down the best trading options further) and is itself part of the broader Business Cycle, which is, in turn, part of the Kondratieff Wave (or cycle).

The Minsky Cycle – coined around the time of the 1998 Russian financial crisis by a guy from PIMCO (Pacific Investment Management Company) – is a key part of the general psychology of trading (which was covered in my first book – *Everything You Need To Know About Making Serious Money Trading The Financial Markets*) and **seeks to chart the nature of the normal life cycle of an economy with particular reference to speculative investment bubbles.**

The idea here is that in times of prosperity, when the cashflow of banks and corporate moves to excess levels (over and above that which is needed simply to pay off debt), a 'speculative euphoria' develops, which soon exceeds that which borrowers can pay off, which, in turn leads to tighter credit conditions etc etc. It is the slow pace at which the financial system moves to at first realise this and then seek to accommodate it that produces a financial crisis; known as the 'Minsky Moment'.

It is interesting to note here that knowing where one is in the cycle is crucial to making long-term, informed and extremely profitable positions, as is illustrated below in the shift along the Minsky Curve of what is propitious and what is not.

Typical Minsky Cycle Characteristics

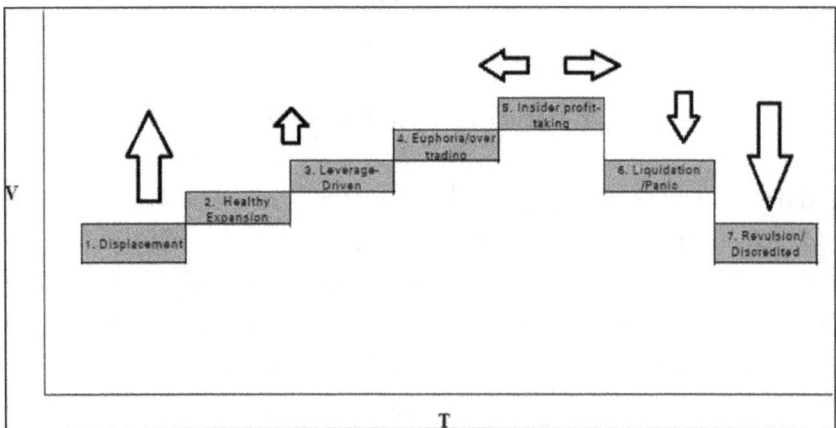

[Chart Key:
V = Values, various assets
T = Time]

So, looking at the above chart, for example, **in the immediate 'displacement' aftermath of the Great Financial Crisis, in the middle or so of 2011, one might have nascent identified pockets of value in Asian FX as various of the countries continued to show exceptional performance**. As the cycle progressed, the major beneficiaries of leverage became certain high-yielding currencies (such as the AUD) and certain commodities (notably, gold).

As credit became easier, so investors became less discerning about the underlying fundamentals of the assets into which they invested, and in the 'euphoria/over-trading' phase, for example poured money into various of the already over-performing equities markets (China springs to mind).

As ever in the markets, key insiders began to twig that a new indiscriminate phase of investment had manifested itself (the "when my gardener is talking to me about stocks then I know it's time to get out" concept), so liquidated out of things like Japanese government bonds and toppish currency positions.

And, once this has occurred, of course, there is a much broader liquidation of assets (at this point it included things like selling USD and gold), which, given the need to make good on losses in margin calls actually involves selling a much broader base of assets than would otherwise be merited.

Finally, the markets reach a point where investors are ultra-cautious in spending their money and regard any asset that is not rated as absolutely solid (CHF is usually a beneficiary of this collective state of mind, of course) as being, in fact, abhorrent, with the main loser at the end of this particular cycle being the debt and other assets of eurozone periphery countries.

Looking at where we were in the middle of 2014, we can see that the displacement macro-shock had been negative rates announced by the ECB, the long and low easing policy of the US Fed appearing to be drawing to an end and a broad-based acceptance of an enduring economic slowdown in China gathering pace.

Within this, different asset classes are at different points along that cycle: for example, the USD may be entering a new long-term uptrend, as mentioned earlier; the JPY appears to be nearing the 'discredited' phase (as dealers cannot see what more can be done to weaken the currency, given what has already been implemented to do so); whilst there has been a generalised liquidation of being long volatility (volatility can be bought or sold, like any other aspect of the market, either directly – say through the VIX and similar indices – or indirectly through proxies).

Given such an identification of which part of the cycle forms the backdrop to your current investment environment, **there are some general inferences that you can take regarding which sectors within – specifically – stock markets may prove the most beneficial at a particular point in time,** as delineated below:

- *Full Scale Recession* (characterised by contracting GDP quarter-on-quarter, falling interest rates, increasing unemployment, declining consumer expectations, among others). Sectors that do well in this environment tend to be: **Cyclicals** (a company's revenues are generally higher in periods of economic prosperity and expansion and lower in periods of economic downturn and contraction, but they can cope easily by reducing wages and workforce during bad times and include companies that produce durable goods, such as raw materials and heavy equipment), **Transports, Technology and Industrials**.

- *Early Recovery* (consumer expectations are rising, unemployment is falling, industrial production is growing and interest rates have bottomed out): **Industrials, Basic materials industry and Energy firms**.
- *Late Recovery* (interest rates can be rising rapidly, consumer expectations are beginning to decline and industrial production is flat): **Energy, Staples and Services**.
- *Early Recession* (Consumer expectations are at their worst, industrial production is falling and interest rates are at their highest): **Services, Utilities, Cyclicals and Transports**.

Risk/Reward Management And Hedging

The Nature Of Risk

For those readers who bought my first book – *'Everything You Need To Know About Making Serious Money Trading The Financial Markets'* – you may wish to skip this section as it is largely a reiteration of what can be found in that book: unless, of course, you have been losing money, in which case you might want to re-read the section properly, possibly with a yellow marker pen in hand.

Ultimately, money goes to where it is best rewarded (yielded from interest rates) for the concomitant risks involved (indicated by credit ratings) and this is, broadly speaking, the definition of the 'risk curve'. **Traders, in order to be successful over time, need to be constantly aware of this risk curve and also to manage the risk/reward ratio of their own investment portfolio in a logical, sensible and emotionless fashion.** Otherwise, they will go broke. It is as simple as that.

The major mistake that traders make is that they get carried away (i.e. let their heart rule their head) with their running positions. Trading is no place for a heart. If you want to spend your days ruled by emotional swings, take lots of drugs, listen to Nirvana and buy a shotgun. Look what it did for Kurt Cobain.

In the case of **in-the-money (ITM) positions,** bad traders (i.e. those not managing their risk properly) exit at the wrong time, either getting out once the peak profit-taking opportunity has passed (through misplaced greed) or getting nervous and taking profit way before they should.

In the case of **out-of-the-money positions (OTM),** in the meantime, they hang on to bad positions hoping that they will turn around. In this latter case, the only real excuse for this hanging on hopefully is if you have invested in sterling and the Governor of the Bank of England personally called you and swore to you on his children's lives – and with a bible in his other hand – that he will be raising UK interest rates by 20% that afternoon, that the budget deficit has been cut to zero unexpectedly, that new figures to be released in the next 10 minutes will show unemployment at 0%, that inflation is stable at a positive rate and that all of the banks have decided to underwrite a sane economic rebound for the country.

If this is not the case then you are guessing, and you might as well take all of the money out of your trading account and give it to a homeless charity because: a. At least it will do some good for others; and b. It will probably do you some good in the longer-term, as on the streets is precisely where you will end up trading in such a manner.

No matter how high-minded one might think oneself, the aforementioned two emotions – greed and fear – are the prevailing ones in trading and despite what Gordon Gekko (whose character, by the way, was reputedly based on an amalgam of one-time junk bond king Michael Milken and corporate raider Ivan Boesky – both of whom went to prison for a while) said, greed is not good and neither is fear.

Greed manifests itself most palpably during bull trends and the less experience/discipline one has, the more one succumbs to its ill-effects on trading strategy. In a bull trend, by definition, there are, in simple terms, more buyers than sellers: which is fine. The problem for the RT comes when he gets greedy for further profits (provided he is long) and decides to hold his position for that bit longer, just to capitalise on his good fortune. The logical outcome of this is that he will hold on to his position until such a point that the trade starts to reverse and go down. Unfortunately, particularly in FX, this turnaround can happen extremely quickly and all the more so if there is a significant presence of hedge fund money in the market.

At this point, the prevailing emotion is still greed, as the trader begins to fret that he has not taken all the profit he could and waits for his position to go back up again to the point at which he could have sold out and taken profit about five minutes earlier. 'Sod's Law' here is that, of course, it will continue to go down, at which point the RT's prevailing emotion starts to change to fear. Fear that he cannot get out of his position except at lower levels and greater fear as all his profit is wiped out and his position starts to go into the red.

By far the best way for a retail trader to avoid being one of the 90% of this breed that loses all his money within 90 days of starting to trade is by utilising – and religiously sticking to – using orders to trade, and we look at this in depth below.

The Risk Curve

The more risk involved in a currency, which broadly acts – along with bonds and equities – as a proxy for the perceived health of the sovereign country of origin, the more reward (interest rate) is required. Hence, the worse an economy is perceived to be doing the more reward investors will want as compensation to hold that currency. And by extension, if that interest rate does not increase then that currency will be unpopular and thus weak.

Having said that, there is a major difference between probability and a risk/reward profile in trading terms.

The law of probability (more accurately, the 'Law of Large Numbers') is:

"If the probability of a given outcome to an event is P and the event is repeated N times then the larger N becomes, so the likelihood increases that the closer, in proportion, will be the occurrence of the given outcome to N*P."

In practical terms, this means really that if you toss a two-sided coin a sufficient number of times then the distribution of the results between heads coming up and tails coming up will be exactly the same.

Right away, I hope, you can see a problem here for the trader. There is a 50/50 chance on the first toss that heads will come up, therefore, according to the logical extension of the other training companies it would be perfectly reasonably to put half your money on heads. You do so and it comes up tails. Oh dear. Nonetheless, according to the aforementioned rationale, you now put everything on heads coming up as given that tails came up first time and the probability of heads coming up was 50% (1 in 2) heads is bound to come up next time. Does it? Of course not. And now you're broke – remember what I said about giving your money to the homeless?

The fact is that probability only does a part of the way to explaining sequences of numbers (which is what any trading actually is).

There is also the random walk theory, in which followers believe that market prices follow a completely random path up and down, without any influence being exerted on them by past price action, making it impossible to predict with any accuracy which direction the market will move at any point or indeed to what degree. However, as we know, this is plainly incorrect, as patterns of all sorts manifest themselves daily, indeed hourly, and all that is required is to know what to look for.

Risk/reward ratios are what you need to know, and that is what we are coming onto.

Risk/Reward Ratios And Basic Effective Order Management

Knowing accurate support and resistance levels is pivotal in determining the risk/reward ratio of a particular trade and in placing orders to capitalise on favourable movements (take-profit orders) or to limit the downside potential of a trade (stop-loss orders).

Technical Analysis (please see *Technical Analysis section* on page 137) is a bit of a self-fulfilling prophecy as whether or not there is any real empirical value in the levels that its classical application produces – the most basic cornerstones being support and resistance levels, as mentioned earlier – the fact that lots of other people believe in it means that these levels take on a trading significance.

Frankly, if everybody thought it was cobblers then, in fact, it would not work. Nonetheless, because people like to see patterns in what is effectively chaos, an understanding of Technical Analysis should be an essential part of everybody's trading armoury nowadays.

One distinct advantage that this 'collective delusion of discerning patterns' means on a day to day basis is that, once you have worked out where the key support and resistance levels really are – and this is a pretty straightforward process – and you have set your risk parameters according to your appetite (in the early days of trading to go for at least a 1 to 4 risk/reward ratio) then you should place your stop-loss orders appropriately and STOP messing around with your trades UNLESS something major happens that invalidates your original hypotheses for undertaking the trades in the first place.

More money has been lost by people messing around with their trades, or trading through boredom, than has ever been lost in rogue trading operations. If you did the Technical Analysis and all the other things that you should have done before entering a trade and nothing extraordinary changes – political, economic, Acts of God – then relax. If you can't relax in front of your screen then leave your orders with your broker/bank/platform and go out to a place where you cannot keep doing daft, unsubstantiated trades because you 'felt like it' or 'were bored' or 'had a hunch' or 'the dog told me to do it'.

USDCAD (1 Year, Daily)

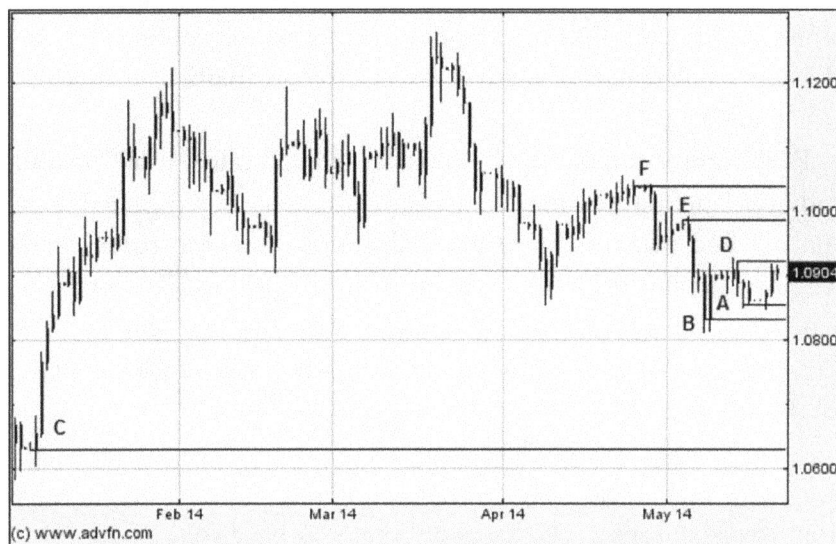

[Chart Key:
A = First support level
B = Second support level
C = Third support level
D = First resistance level
E = Second resistance level
F = Third resistance level]

Net Margin/Trading Requirement (NMR/NTR)

When trading on any platform, **an RT will find that his room for manoeuvre in trading is not only limited by the total amount of capital that he has in his trading account but also by the NMR/NTR of that particular platform**, according to the platform's judgement of the risk involved in any particular asset that he is trading.

For example, even if not trading on any leverage at all (instead, trading £1 per pip meaning £1 gained/lost for each pip gained/lost), one will find that for each £1 traded the platform will reduce one's available account balance by anywhere from £100 to £200 or more, depending upon the type of contract that one has entered into (depending on how risky/volatile the platform assesses each contract to be.

Not only will this eat into your available capital but additionally any losses that a trade occurs as it is ongoing will also be deducted from available capital. So, let us say that you have sold EURUSD at 1.3700 at GBP4 per pip. Even before the pair has moved your capital account will be showing that you are down on available capital by, let us say, GBP800. If you had available capital before trading of £1,000 then you can only afford to have the position go 200 pips against you before you are automatically closed out of the position (and thus wiped out entirely) by the trading platform.

Moreover, it affords you no opportunity for hedging positions as they run (see below). Conversely, of course, if your position makes money from the off then your available capital will increase (although this will not affect the amount that the platform has set aside for your risk margin).

Account Size And Setting Targets

In order to have any peace of mind as a trader, **one requires an account with sufficient capital for one's trading ambitions. Or, conversely, one needs to have trading ambitions that are cut according to one's capital.** One cannot have an imbalance here.

It is true that, with a £500 initial stake in an account, one can, in theory – and no doubt it has been done in practice – become a millionaire within five years (see chart below), if one doubles one's money every six months, as the table below illustrates:

Capital Accumulation Over Six Years From An Initial £500 Investment	
Months	Capital
0	500
6	1000
12	2000
18	4000
24	8000
30	16000
36	32000
42	64000
48	128000
54	256000
60	512000
66	1024000
72	2048000

This, though, requires a high degree of self-discipline, rigorous order management, excellent market knowledge and contacts and highly developed skills of technical analysis (see *Technical Analysis section* on page 137).

In terms of self-discipline first, cut your profit target according to your account balance. As I constantly stress, you should, at minimum, set a risk/reward ratio of 4:1 in the first few years of trading on your own account – that is, for every £1 you might stand to lose you could make £4.

Second, if you are trying to double your money over the 0-6 month period then you must make £500 during that first half year period. Split down £500 into weeks, for a weekly profit target: thus, the weekly profit target for you is £500/26 = £19 per week.

Concomitant with this, you need to work out how much is the maximum that you can place on any one trade. As I have mentioned, professional bank/fund management traders will typically risk anywhere between 1%-5% of their capital on any single trade. I suggest that, to begin with, you risk no more than 1% of your capital on any one trade. Therefore, on any single trade, you can risk no more than £5 in total.

This is clearly not much, if you are doing £1 per pip, which is why I become somewhat irritated by companies who tell you that all you need to start trading is £500. It is true that some trading platforms allow you to trade a minimum lot size of 50p per point, which is one way of circumventing extremely limited capital in an account. Another is to try to trade £1 per pip, but this allows you absolutely no real room for error, as the spread alone (the difference between a trading platform's bid and offer prices for the base currency in a currency pair) is often at least 3 pips. On this basis, you cannot afford for the pair to move more than 2 more pips, which clearly is insane.

Therefore, I would suggest that a **minimum sensible amount to have in a trading account to begin with is between £5000 and £10,000.** This allows you flexibility in hedging ongoing positions that are not performing well in the very short-term but that one believes (based on empirical evidence) will come good in the slightly longer term. And, of course, the doubling process outlined in the earlier chart is still the same.

In order to make £10,000, one must make a weekly profit of £385 per week over six months. 1% of £10,000 is obviously £100, which means that is one's stop-loss. At £1 per pip that is a 100 pip movement against you that is acceptable, which is relatively reasonable in a market of average volatility. Indeed, it may be that, under these conditions, one might consider putting £2 per pip on the trade, whilst simultaneously cutting one's stop-loss to 50 pips from the point of trade entry. As such, it is fairly straightforward and realistic to make the required sum in the target period and even more quickly if using weightings across different asset classes, given proper risk management.

Straight Averaging Up

Given the premise that the aim of trading is to minimise any losses and to maximise any wins, averaging up – if done well – is a good way of achieving the latter.

The basic averaging technique is pretty self-explanatory: it involves **adding to your winning position as the trade continues into profitable territory.** So, for example, in the chart below, you have entered a new position by buying EUR against the USD (selling USD) at 1.3000 – after your technical analysis, you worked out accurately that a break of this key resistance level would indicate a move higher – and have decided to add £1 per pip at every 50 pip upwards increment. Having done this three times, you now have an average long position of £3 per pip at EURUSD1.3050.

EURUSD (5 Years, Weekly)

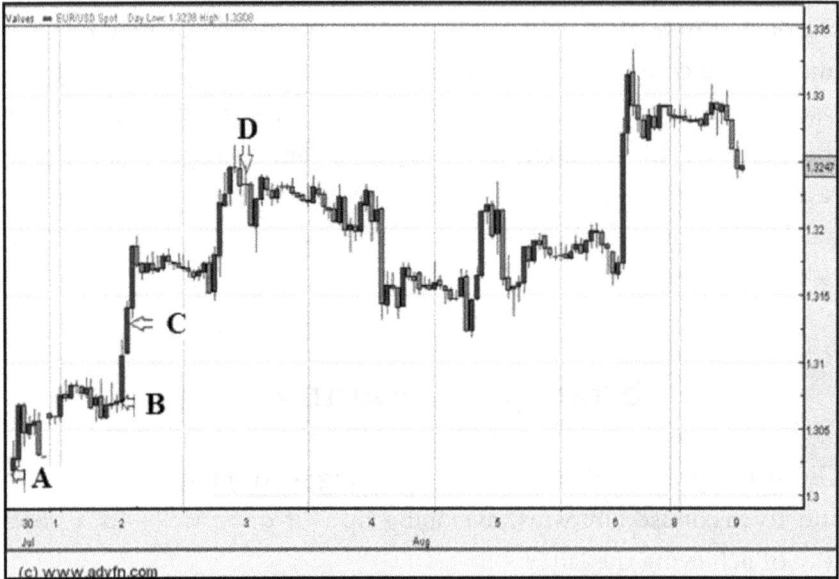

[Chart Key:
A = Buy EURUSD at 1.3000, £1 per pip
B = Buy again at 1.3050, £1 per pip
C = Buy again at 1.3100, £1 per pip
D = Therefore, average long price at £3 per pip is 1.3050]

On £1 per pip at 1.3000, one would have made £250 as the EURUSD hit 1.3250. Another £1 per pip at 1.3050 would have netted a further £200 and the final £1 per pip at 1.3100 a further £150. The total, therefore, would have been £600. Of course, had one put on £3 per pip in the first trade, the profit would have been £750. Additionally the break-even on the trade has now moved up to 1.3050 rather than 1.3000.

If one had not sold at the top of that particular move and the pair had traded down to 1.3100 then one might have lost the third leg profit of £150, which would have resulted in a net profit of just

£150. Also, if the pair had traded back down through the 1.3050 area then one would have incurred a loss on the third long, together with no profit on the second, which would have resulted in a net profit of nothing at all.

Layered Averaging Up

Another way of averaging up that tends against the above phenomenon of being averaged out of any profit is to **add to your long position on pullbacks to the preferred entry level, or the other way around if you are a net seller.** So, if you decide to go long as above then you simply add £1 per pip on any move back towards the 1.3000 level, if you are expecting a sustained move upwards over time.

Such tactics are particularly useful if there is an ongoing struggle between a central bank and a fund on two sides of the trade. For example in USDJPY, after the new Prime Minister Shinzo Abe came to power at the end of 2012, the Bank of Japan has been buying USD and selling JPY very aggressively in order to support its export market (and thus aid broader economic recovery) from around the USD85.50 level, whilst certain funds – especially hedge funds – were selling USD and buying JPY anywhere above 87.00.

Once Abe was more firmly ensconced as PM, this battle moved up the values on USDJPY, as the Bank of Japan was given a much broader policy mandate than before. This was in line with those given to the US Fed and the Bank of England, which included looking at employment rates, interest rates and inflation. In this vein, the banks used quantitative easing (QE) where necessary together with direct currency intervention and Forward Guidance as a means of manipulating their respective currencies.

It was only when, in fact, the Bank of Japan was tasked with ensuring a broad-based policy strategy – engineering sustained nominal annual economic growth of 3% (there has been no average annual nominal GDP growth for 15 years) and at least a 2% annual inflation rate every year from 2015, as well as commencing a massive domestic bond-buying QE programme (Fed-style) – that the JPY managed sustained depreciation of the sort wanted by Abe and moved through the key USDJPY100 resistance level.

Alternately, **adding smaller amounts to the initial position is also a better way in the minds of many to take advantage of further moves** (in the aforementioned case) whilst also limiting the potential – as shown above – for all of one's profits to be eradicated (or even to start making a loss). The converse of this, of course, is averaging down, in which a trader adds to losing positions in the hopes of making money back quicker as the original position reverses.

Value Averaging

As a natural corollary of the above, value averaging is another added value way of managing positions, this time by **constantly readjusting one's risk/reward exposure to a pre-determined level.** Therefore, in practical terms, one sets an amount that falls within one's risk/reward parameters that one wished to have in a particular asset over a particular time.

For example, one may decide that one wishes to have a total exposure per day of £100 in EURUSD, at £1 per pip. In this event, if the position makes £10 in one day then next day one takes the £10 out and still has £100 riding on the position (at the original price). Conversely, if the position loses £10 in one day then the following day one would add another £10 at whatever the new price is to compensate. Thus, one has now spent £110 on the long, albeit it a more favourable average, given a downtrading market.

Trailing Stops

As a position turns into profit, the amount of Net Margin Requirement (NMR)/Net Trading Requirement (NTR) that one has available increases, which can be used either for reinvestment in one of the methods detailed above or can be left where it is, depending on the nature of the market at the time. Nonetheless, depending upon how you manage your position, **there is no point in keeping your stop loss exit order at its original point, but rather you should move it up as the profit margin increases**. This is the notion of trailing stops.

So, basically, if your position increases profit by 10 pips then move your stop up 10 pips and so on.

Hedging

A perfect hedge means one in which no risk whatsoever is taken. As a corollary of this, it means that there will also be no reward. The perfect hedge would be, for instance, buying EURUSD 1mn and simultaneously selling EURUSD 1mn. Thus, perfect hedging is a rather pointless exercise.

Instead, I am interested in a broader sort of hedging that can either help reduce my overall net losses in a bad position (by making offsetting gains in other related areas) or help add to my overall net profits (whilst not actually proportionately increasing the risk involved). In this sense, then, hedging is a method of dynamically managing the risk/reward profile for the trader.

Cross-Currency Hedging

Beginning with the obvious, all currency trades involve buying one currency and selling another.

Let us use EURUSD as the beginning of this example. You are long the EUR, which means you are also short USD: in market code +EURUSD (always mark your position in terms of the base currency first, then the amount (EUR1mn) and then the price (here, 1.5063). Therefore, in market terms you write on your pad: +EURUSD1 @1.5063.)

EURUSD (5 Years, Weekly)

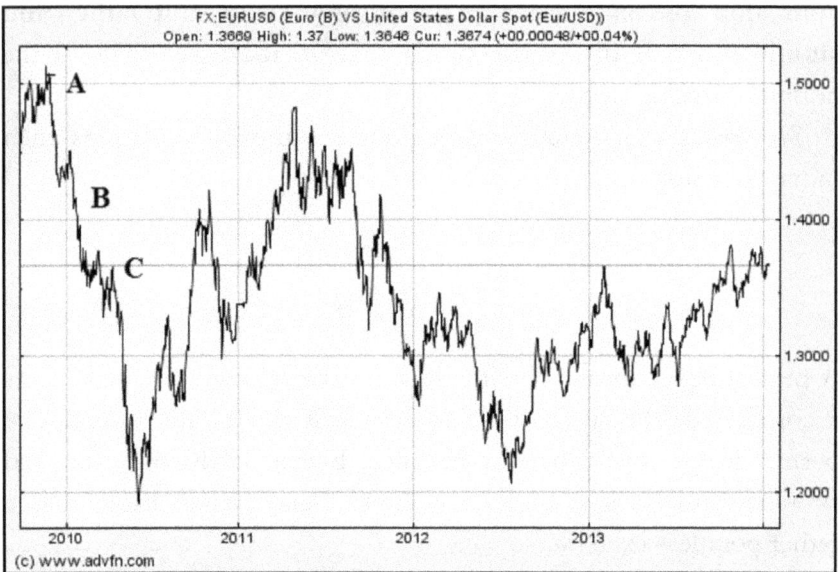

FX:EURUSD (Euro (B) VS United States Dollar Spot (Eur/USD))
Open: 1.3669 High: 1.37 Low: 1.3646 Cur: 1.3674 (+00.00048/+00.04%)
(c) www.advfn.com

[Chart Key:

*A= **Buy euros, 1mn and sell US dollars at 1.5063***

B = *Getting nervous about the euro story, so* **buy US dollars, 1.5mn and sell Swiss francs at 1.0262**

C = *I now have options – I am long EURUSD, long USDCHF, making money on the latter going up as the former goes down.*

Additionally, I can re-weight positions, depending on how each pairing performs (I can, for example, add to my long USDCHF position or reduce my long

EURUSD position) or simply sell EURCHF, as I am effectively net long of that, or I can do counter-balancing stock indices trades]

The market is going against me but I believe (for some good reason) that the EUR will go up soon. However, I am not exactly sure when and how much the swing against me might be. I know that, by definition, if the EUR element of this pair is going down then the USD element of it is going up. Therefore, I can go long the USD against something else to attempt to make money on the rising USD as the EUR goes down, so I go long USDCHF1.5mn as EURUSD breaks through the 1.4750 level.

USDCHF (5 Years, Weekly)

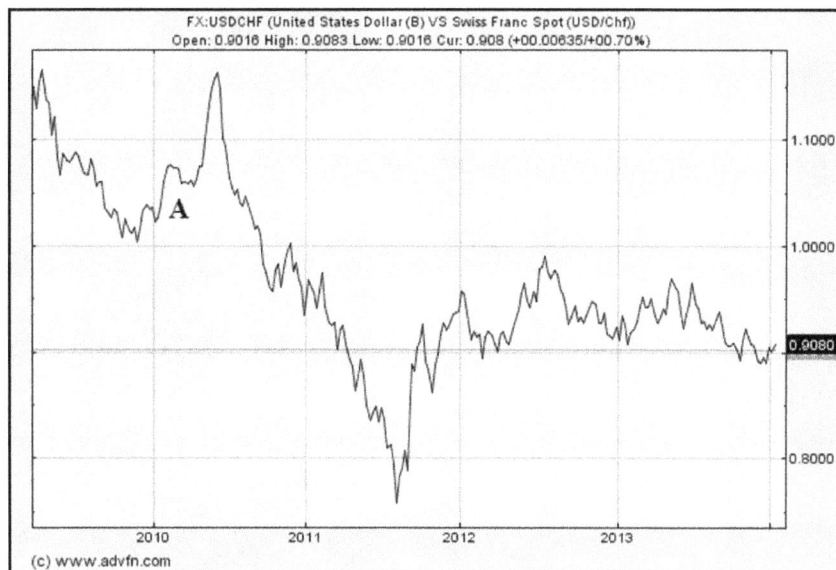

FX:USDCHF (United States Dollar (B) VS Swiss Franc Spot (USD/Chf))
Open: 0.9016 High: 0.9083 Low: 0.9016 Cur: 0.908 (+00.00635/+00.70%)

(c) www.advfn.com

[Chart Key:
A = Buy USD/sell CHF1.5mn at 1.0262]

Now things are looking up, as one is counterbalancing the other almost perfectly, as can be seen from the chart below, given that **I am essentially long EURCHF.**

As the EUR continues in its downward trend I can use some of the averaging techniques described above to help loss turn into profit. This is simply a question of re-weighting each trade. As it stands, I have the same overall capital involved in each trade (EUR1mn or around USD1.5mn) but as the EURUSD continues to trade down, I can add to my long USDCHF position. Let us say that I double it, at 1.0400 to USD3mn for the entire duration of the downtrend in EURUSD, which continues until the beginning of June.

Looking at these trades in P&L terms then:

+EURUSD1mn @ 1.5063, liquidate at 1.1800 = total loss of EUR326,300 (= USD at the new rate = USD385,034).

+USDCHF1mn @ 1.0262, liquidate at 1.1700 = USD143,800

and +USDCHF2mn @ 1.0400, liquidate at 1.1700 = USD260,000.

Therefore, my **total profit for the venture (which did not start out well) was USD77,500.**

EURCHF (5 Years, Weekly)

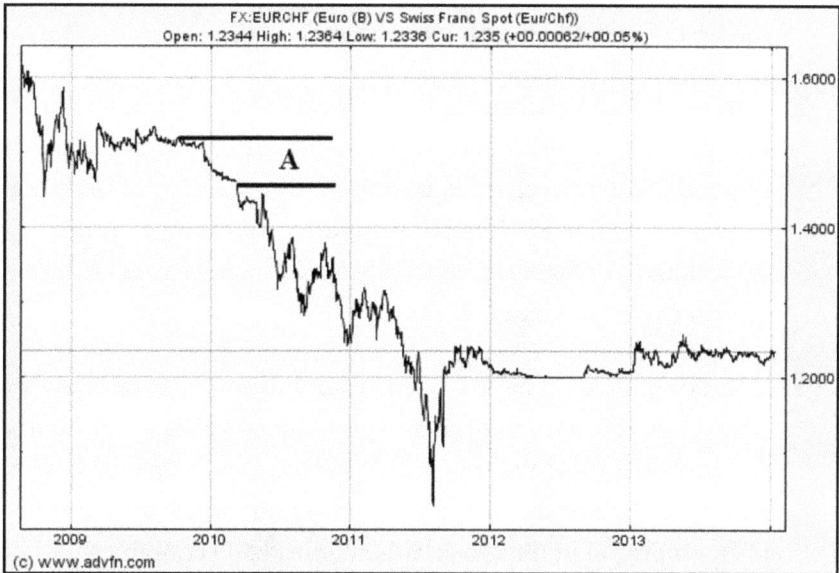

FX:EURCHF (Euro (B) VS Swiss Franc Spot (Eur/Chf))
Open: 1.2344 High: 1.2364 Low: 1.2336 Cur: 1.235 (+00.00062/+00.05%)

[Chart Key:
A = Overall, with just a flat long EURCHF position I am only down 250-300 pips but I can get rid of this entirely by re-weighting]

In the above example, **I could also have sold EURCHF,** which would have given me a flat position, as:

1. +EUR -USD

2. +USD -CHF

3. Therefore, net long EURCHF

4. Therefore, sell EURCHF = flat.

However, there were **many other options available to me whilst I was long EURUSD and long USDCHF:**

1. Increase the relative weighting of the long USDCHF position (as described above) or I could think more laterally still and buy the USD against something else as well.

2. This would have increased my net long USD position but also it would have allowed me to insulate myself against any CHF-specific good news that might cause it to rally and thus lose me money on my long USDCHF position – for example, if the central bank of Switzerland (SNB) raised interest rates unexpectedly or whatever.

3. Therefore, I would have looked around for other currencies where the outlook was grim and good news was not expected on the horizon. At the time, GBP looked especially ropey, with an unpopular government still in power but no clear successor likely to prevail in the General Elections, bad economic numbers, consumer spending still low and so on, so I could have sold GBP and bought USD.

4. This again could be reweighted in terms of amount.

5. And so the process goes on.

Cross-Asset Class Hedging

Sticking with my failing long EURUSD position example for the time being, I need not have just hedged my bets with currencies.

Let us recap on the basic situation: I had gone long EUR, expecting some turnaround in the fortunes of the currency, based perhaps on the notion that future figures might show that the weaker eurozone members (Greece, Spain, Portugal, Italy, Ireland) might be turning themselves around.

So, what else could I do to capitalise on the continued poor performance of the eurozone that is crucifying my long EURUSD position?

1. Sell the major stock indices associated with the individual countries performing especially badly in the EUR region (as shown above).

Greece Athens Stock Exchange (5 Years, Weekly)

Had I sold the ASE as above, say another USD1mn worth, my entry price at the time would have been around 2250 and falling fast. I could also have sold the other major indices of troubled eurozone countries.

2. Looking at it another way, I could have bought US stock indices instead/as well as.

Dow Jones Industrial Average (5 Years, Weekly)

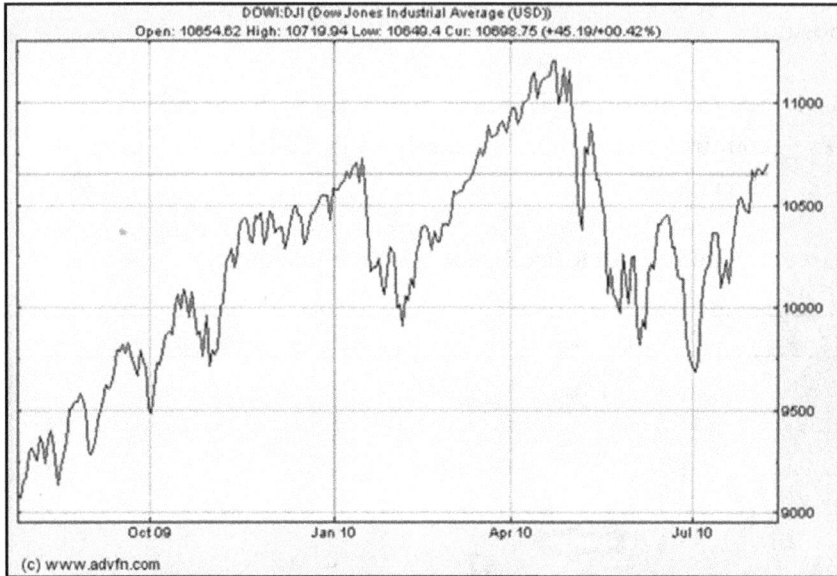

DOWI:DJI (Dow Jones Industrial Average (USD))
Open: 10654.62 High: 10719.94 Low: 10649.4 Cur: 10698.75 (+45.19/+00.42%)

(c) www.advfn.com

3. If I was, in the meantime, suddenly concerned about my net short CHF position then I could hedge out the CHF risk, by buying the major Swiss stock index.

4. I could have done a currency option to hedge risks either side (we will discuss options later on).

Cross-Sovereign/Credit Rating Hedging

Given that the credit risk for the troubled eurozone members was increasing over the period when the EUR was falling out of bed, I could buy credit default swaps (CDS) on the countries worst affected. CDS are basically like insurance policies on entities going bankrupt (for example companies or, in this case, countries). The more technical definition is: CDS pay the buyer face value in exchange for the underlying securities or the cash equivalent should a government or company fail to adhere to its debt agreements. The higher the likelihood, the higher the price of the CDS.

Again, this would have hedged my EUR exposure as, broadly speaking, the more money that I lost on being long EUR, the more money I made on being long Greek CDS (that is, in essence, buying the likelihood of Greece defaulting on its debt).

Summary on Hedging

If one asset is going down then it is extremely likely that another will be going up at the same time in direct proportion, so thinking laterally about all asset markets when one has a position allows you to get out of virtually any bad trade that you have made or to optimise profits on a good one.

Preferably, as discussed elsewhere, you should know all of the possible trading options available to you across as many asset markets as possible before you enter into the trade in the first place.

Options

An option is the right, but not the obligation, to buy or sell an asset at a particular price (the exercise price) on or before a specific future date (the exercise date).

The two most common types of option are called an **American style option** (which can be exercised at any point up to the option expiration date) and a **European style option** (which can only be exercised on the specific exercise date).

(For the more 'exotic' **Asian options** the payoff is determined by the average underlying price over some pre-set period of time, conceptually different from both the American and European option types in which in both cases the payoff of the option contract depends on the price of the underlying instrument at exercise.)

An **option to buy an asset is called a 'call' option and an option to sell one is called a 'put' option. You can buy or sell an option.** If you sell an option then you receive a premium from the buyer (a bit like an insurance premium), however, you are obligated as the seller to pay out to the buyer in the event that the option is exercised (and these payouts can be limitless, depending on how the option has moved).

Options are extremely useful as hedging tools (this was their original purpose, as a type of insurance against unforeseen movements in asset prices) but, as with all financial assets, they can also be used for purely aggressive speculative purposes.

In a currency option, then – let us stick with the EURUSD example that we have been predominantly using in the last few pages – if you bought a EURUSD call then you would be buying the right (but not the obligation) to buy EUR and sell USD, and if you bought a EURUSD put then you would be buying the right (but not the obligation) to sell EUR and buy USD. And vice-versa if you were selling a call or put – you have a liability then to meet the obligation implied in the option if the buyer decides to exercise it.

Although we are not going to go into huge details about the pricing of options, one thing that it is useful to be aware of is that the premium paid to buy an option is a reflection both of the exercise price of the option (and whether it is currently in profit, ITM or out of profit, OTM, see above) and also the volatility of the market for the currency pair.

Looking at options in terms of them being insurance policies is quite helpful in a number of regards. Let us say that you have bought a house and you want to insure its contents against theft for £10,000. The insurance company has to decide on a range of factors in determining the level of your premiums. Have you got window and door locks, are you backing onto a secluded area, is it an area known for burglaries etc? So, let us say that the answers are: yes to locks, no to secluded area, no to burglaries. The insurance company decides that overall you will have to pay them only their £10,000 back over 20 years. This implies zero risk volatility or thereabouts.

One year in and there are a spate of burglaries in the area. Your premiums go up. This is increasing risk volatility and so on and so forth. You have a private security firm patrolling your grounds 24/7, so your premiums go down again due to lower risk volatility.

In the EURUSD example, **the player had gone long EUR short USD at 1.5063 and the position had started to go against him almost from the off. The near-perfect hedge here would have been to buy a EURUSD put (the right but not the obligation to sell EUR and buy USD) at a strike price of 1.5063** although the price would have to be adjusted slightly to take into account the premium that the player would have paid to the seller of the option, but basically you get the idea.

He could, conversely, have banked money in advance if he had sold a EURUSD call option (giving someone the right but not the obligation to buy EUR from the player, therefore the player is selling them and buying USD) also at 1.5063.

There are more interesting ways to actually make money from options, of course, by locking in certain profit zones through a combination of buying and selling calls and puts at different prices, taken together with different hedging techniques, but for the RT it is not especially something they should be considering I would say, certainly not in the first few phases of his development.

A key part of why more investors in general are now looking at options (and futures) investment than were before the new swathe of market regulations (Basel III, Mifid, Dodd-Frank etc), of course, is that they appear to fall outside the confusion of precisely what will and will not be actively managed within the scope of the new FX regulatory environment.

For example, one key idea was that the traditionally bilaterally-traded over-the-counter (OTC) FX derivatives markets would be migrated into a mandatory electronically-executed environment, all under the auspices of central counterparties (CCPs) that act as middlemen between the trading parties and the central clearinghouses. Moreover, participants would be obliged to post initial and variation margin to the CCPs on a daily or intra-day basis, so the need for easily accessible capital to enable such trading would also increase dramatically.

However, timing remains a problem for the futures markets, given that the dates of the contracts are much more specific than those of spot and forward outright contracts, which are completely flexible, and liquidity is also a problem for the futures markets, which are very small compared to the global FX markets.

The massive risk in writing options was highlighted in the Nick Leeson case. Lest we forget the details, first Nick Leeson was in charge of both Barings Bank's front office dealing operations on the Singapore International Monetary Exchange (SIMEX) and its back-office function so that when a trade went wrong at the front end he personally could simply rubber-stamp it at the back end, and he continued to do so until he lost Barings around GBP830mn, bringing the bank down in the process. This being a reminder of over-confidence in one's abilities.

And second, in order to cover his mounting trading losses he decided to write vast numbers of options essentially betting on the Nikkei stock market rising. He had pocketed millions of dollars in 'insurance options' from others and all was looking good as Japan boomed, until the Kobe earthquake hit Japan in January 1995, whereupon the Nikkei fell like a stone and his customer wanted their insurance payments back. Thus illustrating that markets are not always predictable.

In sum, be very careful indeed, when thinking about using options.

Technical Analysis

Candlesticks

For those readers who bought my first book – *'Everything You Need To Know About Making Serious Money Trading The Financial Markets'* – you may wish to skip this section as it is largely a reiteration of what can be found in that book: unless, of course, you have been losing money, in which case you might want to re-read the section properly, possibly with a yellow marker pen in hand.

This method of charting is particularly useful as it not only shows simply whether the market has largely bought the base currency (typically shown in green or white) or sold it (typically shown in red or black) but also how strong these buys or sells were (indicated by the length of the lines above each candle, 'wick', for buying or below, 'shadow', for selling).

Candlestick Structure

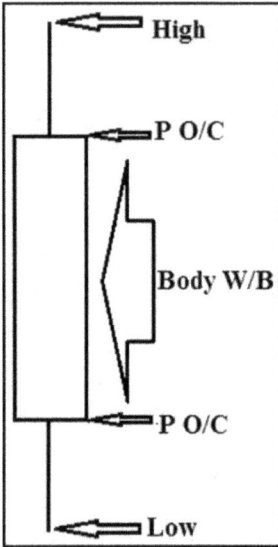

[Chart Key:
High = Highest price during trading time period
P O/C = Trading time period open or close price
Body W/B = Real body is white (or green) if currency closed higher over the
trading period or black (or red) if it closed lower
P O/C = Trading time period open or close price
Low = Lowest price during trading time period]

If a market is undecided as to where it views the direction of a pair then the candlestick will have no substantial body, wick or shadow (**'doji'**), reflecting that the price closed the day where it opened and that neither buyers ('bulls') nor sellers ('bears') prevailed in moving the pair their way over the course of the trading hours.

A similar inference can be taken from the **'Spinning Top'** pattern, although not to quite the same degree, as some intra-day movement will have taken place. In either event, both can be viewed as **marking possibly the end of the previous trend,** as it has run out of steam. These patterns make ideal places to enter new trades or exit existing ones.

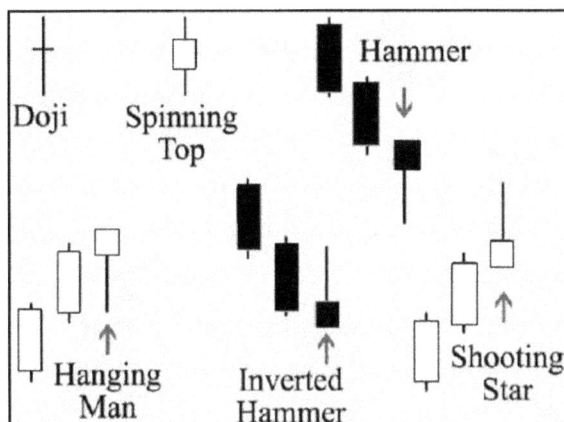

The 'Hammer' pattern appears after a previous move to the downside and indicates that a move to the upside is on the cards. The long shadow shows that, despite it trading substantially lower during the day, the weight of selling was not sufficient for it to stay at depressed trading levels. Consequently, the inference is that major buyers have stepped in at these levels and may well continue buying overnight or as the new Western trading period properly commences.

The same can be said for the 'Inverted Hammer', although to a lesser degree, as, although buyers have stepped into the market, they have failed, on this occasion, to reverse the downtrend entirely.

Conversely, the 'Shooting Star' should be read as a sign that a move to the downside is on the cards, after a previous move to the upside, with bulls having failed to continue to push the pair higher and substantial bears having now entered the market.

The same can be said for the 'Hanging Man' although to a lesser degree, as, although sellers have stepped into the market, they have failed, on this occasion, to reverse the uptrend entirely.

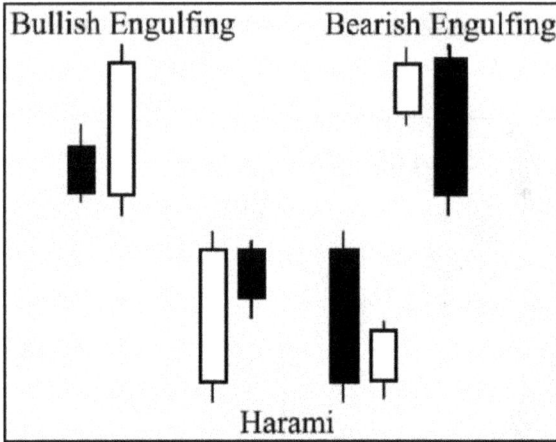

A '**Bullish Engulfing**' pattern is a clear indication that the signs of reversal of a previous trend (either through a Shooting Star or Hanging Man) have gained momentum, and the reverse is true of the '**Bearish Engulfing**' pattern (either through the Hammer or Inverted Hammer).

The '**Harami**' pattern, though, which can occur after a move either up or down, can be taken again as a sign of uncertain price follow-through and may mark the beginning of a change of trend direction.

USDCAD (1 Year, Daily)

FX:USDCAD (United States Dollar (B) VS Canadian Dollar Spot (USD/Cad))
Open: 1.0944 High: 1.0991 Low: 1.0933 Cur: 1.0949 (+00.0005/+00.05%)

(c) www.advfn.com

[Chart Key:
H = Hammer
BE = Bullish engulfing
SS = Shooting star
BeE = Bearish engulfing
STs = Spinning tops
O = Overall uptrend
I = Indecision of the market]

In all of the above cases, the **weight that one should attach to these patterns should be increased when additional confirmations are found**.

These can be where they occur at **major resistance and support levels, Fibonacci levels** (key mathematical ratios of an original number, representing a move up or down: 23.6%, 38.2%, 50% and 61.8%) or **Moving Average** levels (simply, each day's price added together and then divided by a certain number of days: 20, 50 and 100 are the most used), including selected oscillators.

In the above chart, for instance, aside from a few moves down (which fail to gather momentum, as indicated by the Spinning Top patterns) all of the significant moves have been to the upside (as indicated by the rolling Hammer patterns).

USDCAD (1 Year, Daily)

FX:USDCAD (United States Dollar (B) VS Canadian Dollar Spot (USD/Cad))
Open: 1.0944 High: 1.0991 Low: 1.0933 Cur: 1.0958 (+00.0014/+00.13%)

(c) www.advfn.com

[Chart Key:
F1 = Fibonacci level 1, 23.6%
F2 = Fibonacci level 2, 38.2%
F3 = Fibonacci level 3, 50.0%]

Interestingly here, though, it can be seen that the Moving Averages and the Fibonacci levels have acted both as support and resistance levels at various times throughout the trading cycle, and where these have occurred concomitant with the candlestick patterns as described above, they have led to a sustained move in whichever direction they pointed.

Resistance And Support Levels

Support levels (where the market has overwhelmingly bought the base currency in the past, once it has been in decline) will invariably be found **below the current market price**, whilst **resistance levels** (where the market has overwhelmingly sold the base currency in the past, once it has been on the rise) will be found **above the current market price**.

In other words, in chart terms, support levels can be found where selling turns to buying (denoted on candlestick charts, see below, as a red bar turning to green), whilst resistance levels can be found where buying turns to selling (denoted on candlestick stick charts as a green bar turning to red). R1 is the first resistance level and so on, whilst S1 is the first support level, with the current market price indicated in the black box.

EURUSD (1 Year, Daily)

FX:EURUSD (Euro (B) VS United States Dollar Spot (Eur/USD))
Open: 1.3678 High: 1.3679 Low: 1.3579 Cur: 1.3588 (-00.00897/-00.66%)

R2
1.3800
R1
S2
S1
1.3588
1.3400
Nov 18   Dec 1   Dec 16   Jan 1
(c) www.advfn.com

[Chart Key:
S1 = First support level
S2 = Second support level
R1 = First resistance level
R2 = Second resistance level]

These levels should be the cornerstones of all serious trading activity, as they act (together with other confirmations, discussed below) as signals to buy or sell into a new position or to exit existing ones.

To reiterate, though, **it is essential to note that resistance and support levels do not always coincide with any/all of these additional confirmation signals**. It may well be, for example, that a particular level has been **targeted by a country's central bank** as being essential for the advancement of its economic or monetary policy and that it will act decisively to ensure either that its currency weakens at a certain level (to encourage exports and boost economic growth, for instance) or strengthens (to discourage demand-led inflation, for instance).

The chart below, for example, shows the determination of the Bank of Japan (always one of the more active global central banks) stepping in to prevent the JPY from strengthening to such a degree that the country's exports would become even more uncompetitive in the world's markets than already was the case at the time.

USDJPY (5 Years, Weekly)

[Chart Key:
R1 to R10 = The sequentially lower resistance levels hit by serious hedge funds and others, from longs taken out all the way down, before the Bank of Japan effectively set a floor]

Similarly, it may be that there are enormous **FX options** that would be triggered if a currency reached a certain level. In this case, whomever held the option would do everything cost-effective that they could to prevent it reaching the strike price for the option.

Often, one will see levels that apparently have little or no other obvious significance being resolutely defended up to a certain date (the expiration date for the option) and then dramatically going through that level once the option has lapsed, as shown below.

USDCAD (5 Years, Daily)

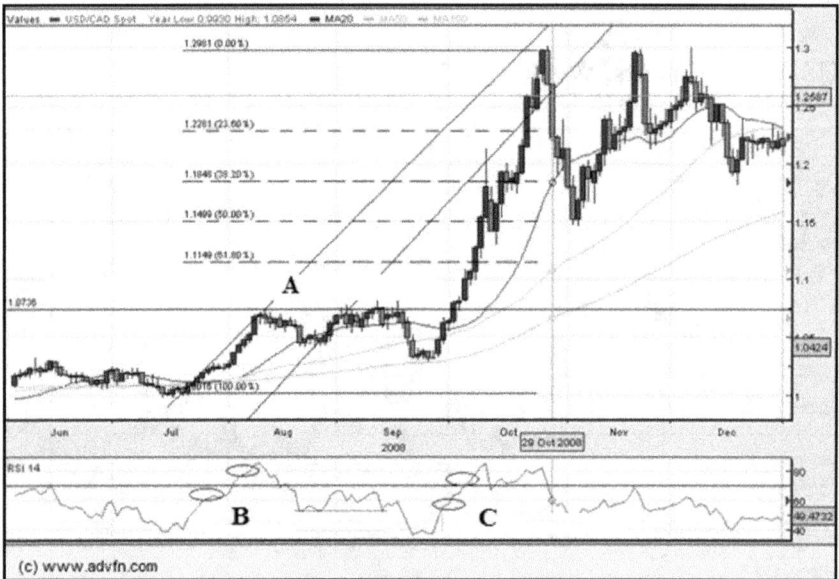

[Chart Key:
A = USD call, CAD put option @ 1.0745
B = Big buying but capped
C = Big buying not capped]

Fibonacci Levels

These are key mathematical ratios of an original number (price), representing a move up or down: **23.6%, 38.2%, 50% (not actually**

a Fibonacci ratio, but most Fibonacci users include it anyhow), 61.8% and 100%.

These can be overlaid on a chart, from the bottom of a trend to the top in a bullish market or from the top of a trend to the bottom in a bearish one.

As mentioned earlier, they can often mark resistance and support levels, as shown below.

US Dow Jones Industrial Average (5 Years, Weekly)

[Chart Key:
A = 23.6% Fib level acts as support
B = 38.2% Fib level acts as resistance
C = 50% Fib level acts first as support and then as resistance]

In the above chart, we see clearly the **correlation between Fibonacci levels and those of support and resistance.** Interestingly here we also see that at the 50% level, initially this starts out as a resistance but then, as the cycle progresses, it acts as a support.

Moving Averages

These are particularly useful in determining short-term indications as to whether a market is set to continue in its current trend, reverse that trend or trade in a range. As mentioned earlier, MAs are simply each day's price added together and then divided by a certain number of days: 20, 50 and 100 are the most used.

As an additional confirmation (to established support and resistance levels, for instance), they offer a good idea of whether a currency is likely to break to the topside or the downside, as illustrated below.

USDJPY (5 Years, Weekly)

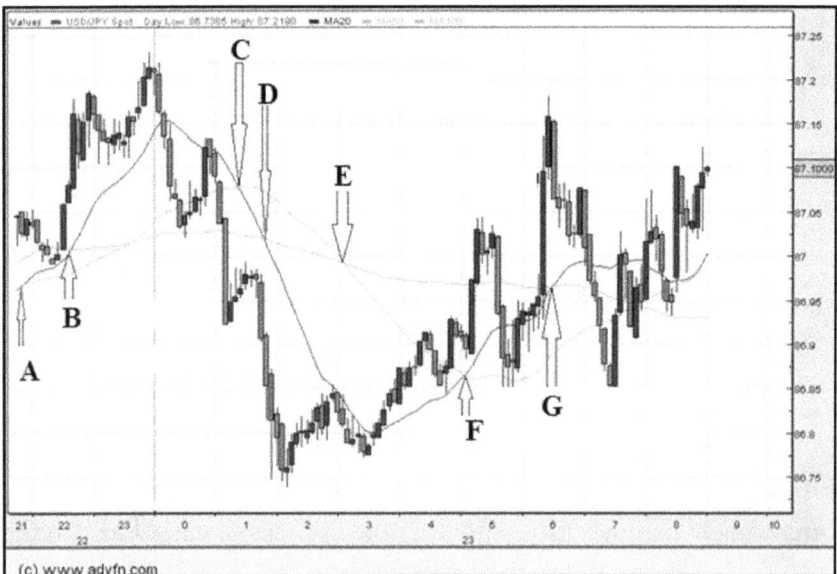

[Chart Key =
A = MA20 up through MA50 = BUY
B = MA20 through MA100 = BUY
C = MA20 down through MA50 = SELL
D = MA20 down through MA 100 = SELL
E = MA50 down through MA100 = OVERSOLD
F = MA20 up through MA100 = BUY
G = MA20 through MA50 = BUY]

Broadly speaking, as shown above, if the short-term MA20 breaks through a longer-term MA then one might expect the currency pair to trade in whichever direction that break has occurred. More helpfully still, MAs can be used for earlier trading indications, using the **Moving Average Convergence-Divergence** (MACD) indicator, as shown below.

USDJPY (5 Years, Weekly)

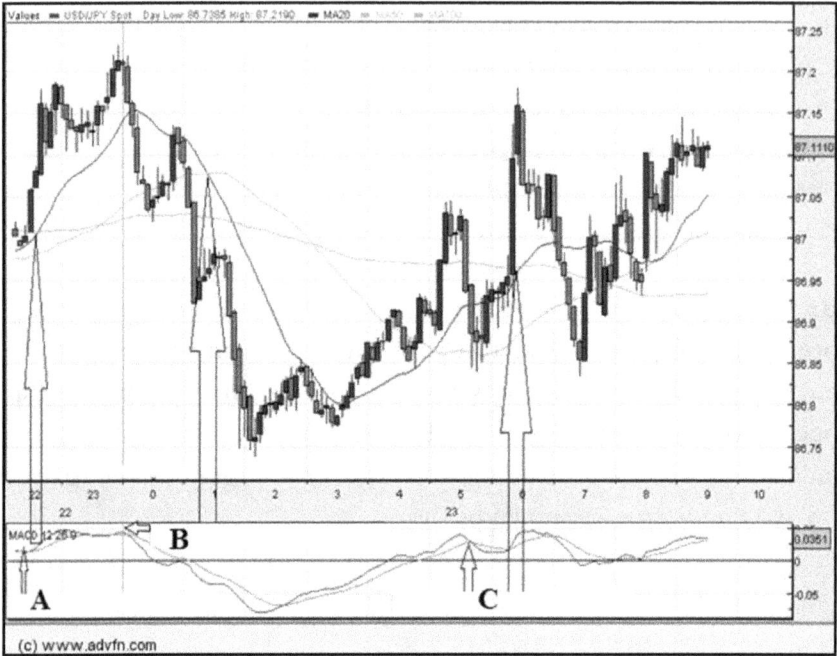

[Chart Key:
A = Early signal for crossover = BUY
B = Early signal for crossover = SELL
C = Early warning for crossover = BUY]

MAs are also a vital part of determining the momentum of a price movement, in its application with the 3/10 Oscillator. This is a simple indicator constructed by subtracting the 10 day period Exponential Moving Average from the 3 day period Exponential Moving Average (but do not fret, virtually all charting packages allow one to replicate this with the MACD by setting the short term parameter to 3, the long term parameter to 10 and the smoothing parameter to 1.

Dow Jones Price/Oscillator Convergence/Divergence Signals

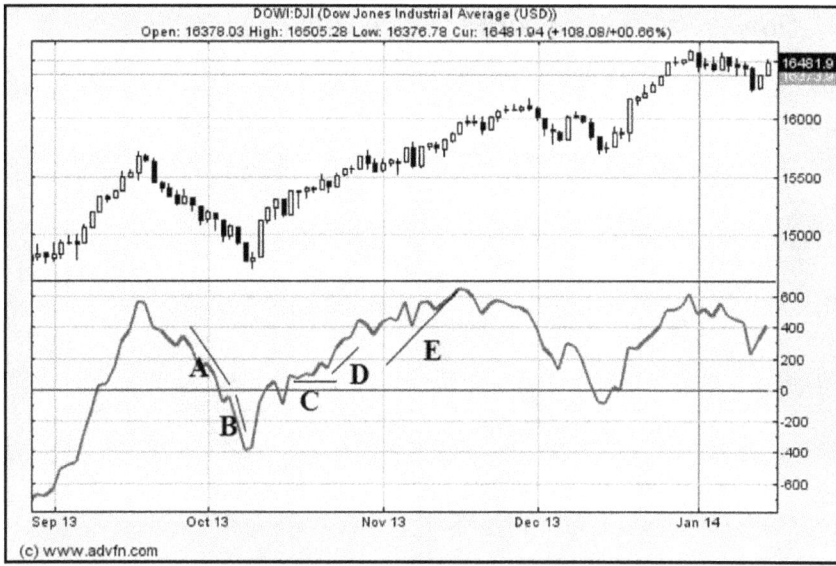

[Chart Key:
A = Selling momentum gathers force
B = Selling momentum diverges = change of direction due
C = Range trading momentum
D = Buying momentum kicks in
E = Buying momentum gathers force]

Anyhow, the concept underlying this indicator (similar in theory to the RSI) is that if a price move up or down and is expected to be sustained then one would anticipate that, along with a range of higher highs (for an upmove) or lower lows (for a downmove), the momentum (or force) behind each of these would also be sustained. If not, one would have to question whether the move can have the strength (more buyers than sellers or the other way around) to continue.

Dow Jones Bearish Regular Divergence Of Price/Oscillator

= Although the price is rising, momentum is going down = bearish divergence

[Chart Key:
A = Higher high
B= Lower high]

Dow Jones Bearish Hidden Divergence Of Price/Oscillator

= The price is still bid, but at a lower level, and momentum is gaining at lower prices

[Chart Key:
A = Lower high
B = Higher high]

Dow Jones Bullish Regular Divergence Of Price/Oscillator

= Although the price is falling, there is less momentum pushing it down

[Chart Key:
A = Lower low
B = Higher low]

Dow Jones Bullish Hidden Divergence Of Price/Oscillator

= *Although it is still offered, the momentum gains as the price rises relatively*

[Chart Key:
A = Higher low
B = Lower low]

Relative Strength Index (RSI)

RSI is another extremely useful oscillator indicator. **In general terms, the RSI shows the momentum of a pair's trading – in effect, the degree of market participation in its current price movement – and can act as a valuable pre-emptive indicator showing a potential reversal of trend.**

For example, even if a pair appears to be rising quickly, if the RSI is showing that negative momentum is occurring then it might be time to look at the other indicators that signalled a long position and look to either exit an existing long or establish a new short.

Conversely, as shown in the chart below, there is a very notable shift upwards in RSI higher before the actual market price follows it.

EURUSD (1 Year, Daily)

= RSI confirms upward trend before actual price turns higher

FX:EURUSD (Euro (B) VS United States Dollar Spot (Eur/USD))
Open: 1.3604 High: 1.363 Low: 1.3584 Cur: 1.3617 (+00.00134/+00.10%)

(c) www.advfn.com

[Chart Key:
A = RSI rises sharply higher, in advance of the price movement
B = Actual market price catches up with bullish momentum on RSI]

More specifically, the RSI moves between a scale of 0 to 100, with 100 showing that every participant in the market is buying the base currency of a pair and 0 showing the opposite. **As a rule of thumb, any reading of 70 and above indicates that the pair is overbought, with a possible reversal on the cards, and any reading under 30 showing it is oversold and that the opposite is**

true. This, together with the formations of usual double top/bottom patterns, can show up even before they do in the actual price movement ('Divergence').

Similarly, areas of support and resistance show up very clearly on RSI patterns, as shown below.

EURUSD (1 Year, Daily)

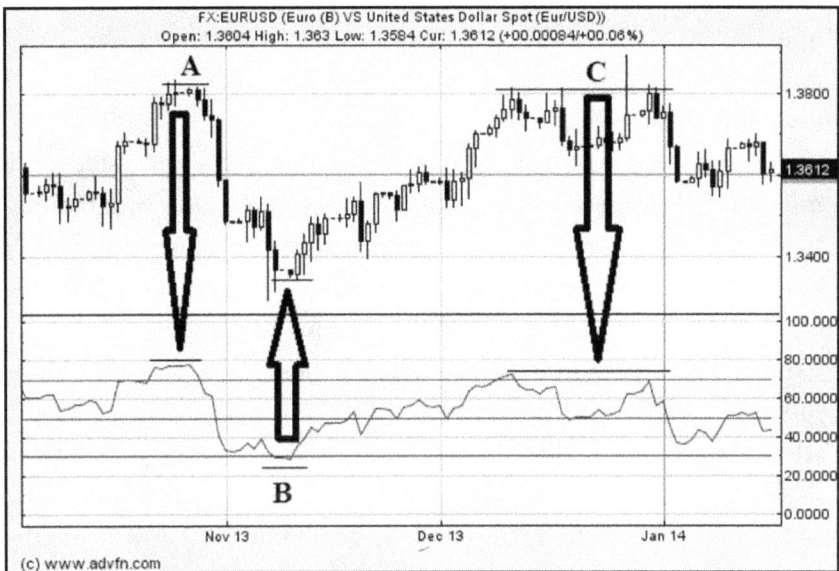

[Chart Key:
A = RSI shows genuine resistance level in the price, in advance
B = RSI shows genuine support level in the price, in advance
C = RSI shows genuine rolling resistance level]

As is evident from the above, RSI's principal use is not in already trending markets, in which it can be used as a confirmation of direction or as an early warning indicator of a change of direction (if above 70 or below 30) but rather in range-bound markets looking for direction.

Here, as shown above, it can act as a proxy for volume interest in particular positions, so that, for example, a sharp spike up in RSI in a market trading around the mid-level could be taken as an early signal of a bullish move and vice-versa.

Bollinger Bands

Right up front I should say that, personally, I am not a big fan of these, but some people set some store by them, so I thought that I should cover them. So, here we go.

Bollinger bands are plotted an equal distance either side of a simple moving average. The default settings on trading programmes use a 20 period simple moving average with the upper band (UB) plotted 2 standard deviations above the moving average and the lower band (LB) plotted 2 standard deviations below it.

In periods of low price volatility, these standard deviations become smaller (this process is called a 'squeeze' in Bollinger parlance) than in periods of high volatility and vice-versa (a 'bubble').

Given this, there is undoubtedly money to be made from anticipating/participating in such a breakout/breakdown to the existing bands.

EURUSD (1 Year, Daily)

FX:EURUSD (Euro (B) VS United States Dollar Spot (Eur/USD))
Open: 1.3604 High: 1.363 Low: 1.3584 Cur: 1.3615 (+00.00114/+00.08%)

[Chart Key:
A = Squeeze
B = Bubble
C = Upper band acts as resistance level
D = Lower band acts as support level]

More appositely, it is better to use Bollinger bands together with other firmer indicators such as support and resistance levels, Fibonacci levels and so forth, and to use them in such a way as to modify the results with what the Bollinger bands tell you about the probability of a move continuing/reversing.

If the price is moving towards the top of a band then beware longs, and if it is moving towards the bottom of a band then beware shorts. But don't get too hung up on what Bollinger Bands say in and of themselves.

Elliott Wave Theory

The market consists broadly of two types of investors: **institutional ones (huge) and retail ones (small)**. The general parameters of this investment universe are simple enough: in 2009, it was measured that retail traders (RT) on average are responsible for about USD110bn in currency flows across options, swaps, futures and spot forex in total per day; the figure for institutional investors (II), though, was around USD3.2trn, and although the total turnover figure increased in the 2013 BIS FX Survey, the counterparty proportions remained essentially the same.

It is against this backdrop that Elliot Wave Theory is particularly useful as it shows major moves and minor ones, with the former likely to be caused by IIs (and well worth following, if they are not spoofs) and the latter likely to be caused by RTs playing catch-up (normally a good time to start thinking about exiting a trade).

In its most basic form, Elliott Waves show that the market does not move in a completely chaotic fashion but rather is a product of patterns that repeat themselves over time. These patterns ('waves') define a trend, which can be the basis for predictive trading.

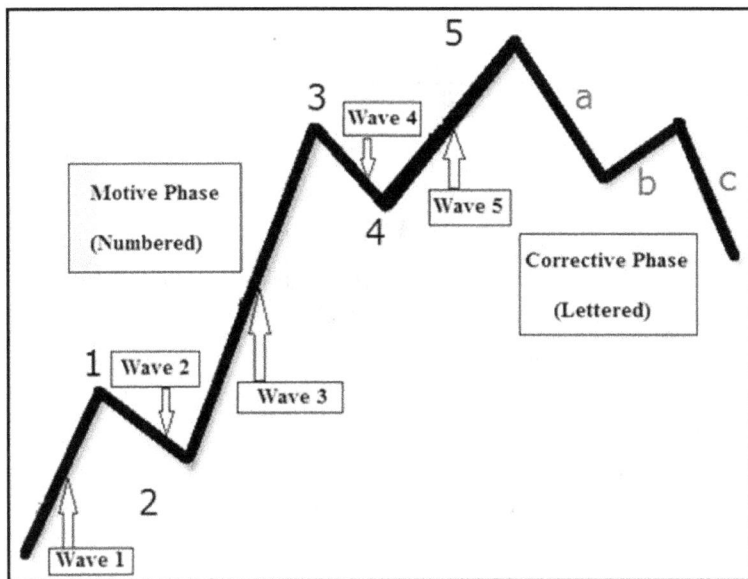

[Chart Key:
See text below for 'Motive' and 'Corrective' definitions]

More specifically, according to Elliott (Ralph Nelson Elliott, just in case you were wondering, who posited his theory in around 1934), a trending market moves in a **five-three wave** pattern, where the first five waves ('motive waves') move in the direction of the larger trend. Following the completion of the five waves in one direction, a larger corrective move takes place in three consecutive waves ('corrective waves'), as illustrated in the above chart.

Interestingly, **the patterns identified by Elliott occur across multiple time frames**: that is, a completed five wave sequence on a small time frame (5 minutes, for instance) may well be just the first wave of a longer temporal sequence (in a daily chart, for example) and so on and so forth.

Elliott Waves On EURUSD

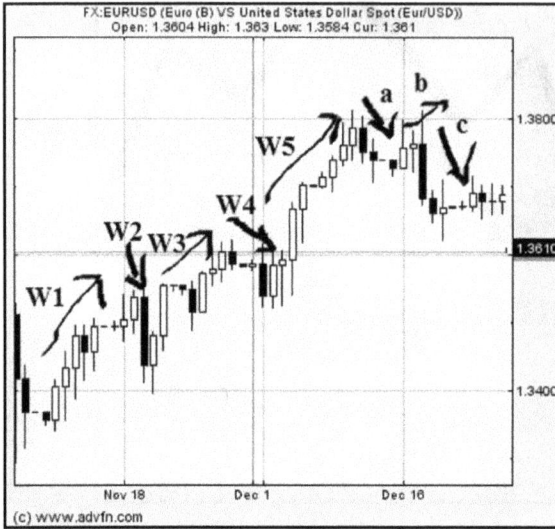

[Chart Key:
W1 to W5 = Motive phase waves
A to c = Corrective phase waves]

The **combination of Elliott Waves and Fibonacci ratios is particularly useful in trading into new positions or trading out of existing ones for a number of reasons**, outlined as follows: Fibonacci ratios are usually important levels of supply and demand (ie, support and resistance).

The motive and corrective levels are often measured by percentages of the previous wave length, with the most common levels being the Fibonacci ones of 38%, 50%, 61.8% and 100%; timings with a distance of 13, 21, 34, 55, 89 and 144 periods should be particularly monitored (e.g., if you find a crucial reversal or an unfolding of a pattern on a daily chart then expect another crucial unfolding at the above daily points thereafter); a corrective move that follows a motive move from a significant low or high usually retraces 50% to 61.8% of the preceding impulse; wave 4 usually corrects as far as 38.2% of wave 3; given that wave 2 generally does not overlap the start of wave 1 (ie, the 100% of it), the start of wave 1 is an ideal level to place stops; and the target of wave 5 can be calculated by multiplying the length of wave 1 by 3.236 (2 X 1.618).

Continuation Patterns

These patterns allow the trader not only to understand from where the price action and momentum has come but also to anticipate where and to what degree it is headed. Thus, as these patterns are also watched by thousands of other traders around the globe, they allow an RT to obtain an ongoing record of the sentiment surrounding a currency pair at any given time and consequently allow the trader to manage his order placing better as well.

Ascending And Descending Triangles

Triangles basically allow the trader to gauge which of the myriad support and resistance levels on a chart are the ones he should be watching most carefully in determining false or genuine breakouts.

An **ascending triangle** is formed by a combination of diagonal support and horizontal resistance, implying that the bulls are gaining the upper hand in the ongoing trading dynamic of the pair and buying at higher and higher levels, while the bears are merely trying to defend an established level of resistance.

EURGBP (1 Year, Daily) Ascending Triangle

FX:USDCAD (United States Dollar (B) VS Canadian Dollar Spot (USD/Cad))
Open: 1.0932 High: 1.0963 Low: 1.0917 Cur: 1.0924 (-00.00083/-00.08%)

A

B

2011   2012   2013
(c) www.advfn.com

[Chart Key:
A = Horizontal resistance level
B = Inclining support]

Clearly, in the above example, the trader has advanced warning that the pair is more likely to break up through the resistance level than down through the support one. Also, of course, by anticipating the formation of the triangle the trader can gain/not lose further points, depending on his position, as currency pairs often trend, consolidate and then re-trend.

In the case of a **descending triangle**, the bears are gaining strength and selling at lower and lower levels, while the bulls are merely trying to defend an established level of support.

AUDUSD (1 Year, Daily) Descending Triangle

FX:AUDUSD (Australian Dollar (B) VS United States Dollar Spot (Aud/USD))
Open: 0.8916 High: 0.8916 Low: 0.8772 Cur: 0.8784 (-00.01316/-01.48%)

[Chart Key:
A = Declining resistance
B = Horizontal support]

**Given these two scenarios, it is easy to see that one can make
money rising the principal wave up or down respectively and
also to see that triangles make the placement of stop loss orders
relatively simple as well;** in the ascending triangle example, they
would be placed just under the inclining support line at a level that
accorded with one's own risk/reward ratio for a rolling long position.

Conversely, in the descending triangle example, they would be
placed at a point above the declining resistance level that accorded
with one's own risk/reward ratio for a rolling short.

In the cases of both ascending and descending triangles, **any true
break (more than one spoof break-out) of its direction (up for
descending triangles, down for ascending ones) should be**

taken seriously by traders to consider exiting trades made on the trend until that point (taking profit) and reversing positions.

Flags

Flags and pennants generally represent a pause in trend and can be used either to take profits on a position going with that trend or to add to that trending position, if one is feeling particularly aggressive (and, preferably, has one's confidence bolstered by other factors meriting an increase in position size – more favourable than expected fundamental or political developments, for example).

The example below is of a downward trending USDJPY, which pauses for consolidation in a flag pattern, before resuming its downward trajectory. Often one can expect pretty much the same number of pips in the second part of the downtrend (labelled 'Downtrend 2' in the chart, appositely enough) as in the first part of the downtrend (you can work out what this one is labelled), but in the chart below, it seems on cursory glance that this is not the case.

However, looking further into the distance and going on the basis of a longer-term trade, it becomes apparent that, in fact, the real second wave (or you could term it 'Downtrend 2, Part 2) makes up the entire pips expected as a result of Downtrend 1.

USDJPY (5 Years, Weekly) Flag In A Downtrend

[Chart Key:
A = Downtrend 1 = 723 pips
F = Flag
B = Downtrend 2 = 348 pips, OR DOES IT? See Below]

In fact, this flag and many similar presage a much sharper move down, as can be seen below.

USDJPY (5 Years, Weekly) Extended Continuation In A Downtrend

[Chart Key:
F = Flag from previous chart
A = Logical conclusion of the original downtrend 1 = 700 pips had the trade been stuck with]

Trend Reversals – Double Top/Bottom And Head And Shoulders Patterns

Given that the market has a way of generally correcting any untoward excessive movements one way or another in asset prices over time, spotting a real reversal in a trend from just a shimmering mirage is key to making money on a long-term basis.

In this respect, we have already covered a lot of ground, but there are a couple of other, more basic patterns that a trader should look out for.

A **Double Top is, as it sounds, when prices stop rising at the same point twice in a short sequence of time**, as shown below. In order for a real reversal of trend to be indicated, the pair must break down through the key support level as indicated on the chart. This is sometimes the result, as we have also touched on, of a central bank looking to halt the appreciation of its currency to such a degree that its export revenue is damaged (or, indeed, of financial institutions guarding a level in order not to be hit by an option being exercised).

GBPUSD (1 Year, Weekly) Double Top

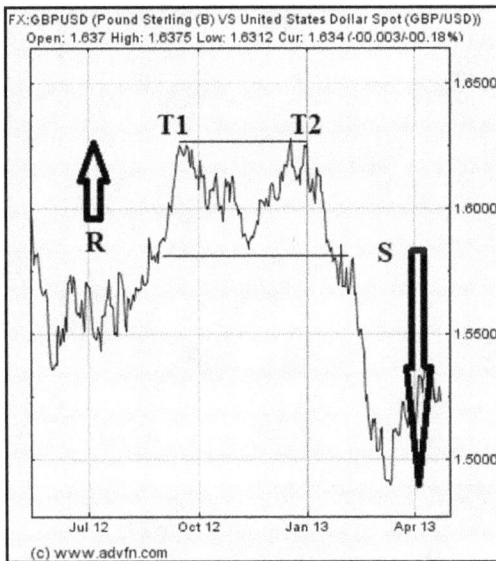

FX:GBPUSD (Pound Sterling (B) VS United States Dollar Spot (GBP/USD))
Open: 1.637 High: 1.6375 Low: 1.6312 Cur: 1.634 (-00.003/-00.18%)

(c) www.advfn.com

[Chart Key:
R = Rising trend
T1 = First top
T2 = Second (double) top
S = Break below this double support level here implies downtrend]

A double bottom is the same principle, only reversed.

In the meantime, a head and shoulders pattern, as illustrated below, develops with the exchange rate trending up and forming the left shoulder on a reversal. Then the market trends higher to form the head and falls back to the same support of the first shoulder to form the right shoulder. The neckline is thus the line connecting the troughs between the peaks. If it is broken, expect a downside move to occur.

AUDUSD (1 Year, Daily) Head And Shoulders Trend Reversal Pattern

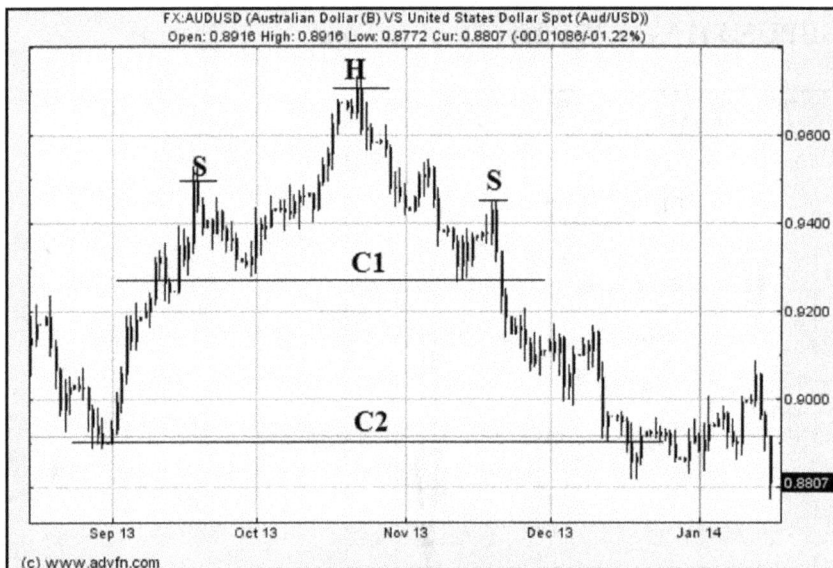

[Chart Key:
S = Shoulder
H = Head
C1 = Confirmation of breakdown 1
C2 = Confirmation of further breakdown 2]

Summary

Develop your own set of key indicators that you have learnt to combine in such a way that you can trust yourself to interpret them sufficiently well to make money more often that you lose it.

Do not stick every available indicator on a chart, as you will just confuse yourself and lose money.

Personally, despite having done this for over 20 years, I consider a likely winning trade as having as many as possible of the **'Perfect Seven'** attributes which are:

1. Know where the **correct support and resistance levels** are located over different trading periods (1 hour, 1 day, 1 month, 1 year are a good start).

2. Pick out the **overall longer-term trend** to follow, as dictating your overall strategy, whilst also making short-term profits by jobbing in and out of the market (based on shorter-term signals, such as MACD and RSI).

3. Look carefully at the **Fibonacci elements** in a trade, using intra-trend Fibonacci levels well.

4. Watch out for **multiple confirmation areas** (for example, where support and resistance levels are also Fibonacci levels, important MAs and crossovers and so forth).

5. **Talk to a select group of other traders** (maximum, I suggest, is three and preferably still in a major bank/fund management dealing room) to get an idea of where the major orders have been placed by the big institutions.

6. Know everything you can about the **fundamental economic and political situations** in countries the currencies of which

you will be trading and those outside (in trading, everything is connected).

7. Monitor **developing trends in all the major asset classes**, in order to anticipate coming trends in the particular markets in which you are focused.

With this backdrop in place, manage orders sensibly. Decide where the stop-loss and the take-profit should be (based on one's own risk/reward ratio) then stick to them.

Sticking to whatever methodology one has, provided it is sound, and to one's order levels (and thus risk/reward ratio levels) will mean that one has more free time away from just sitting staring at a screen, that one will make money over time and that one will not go completely bonkers.

Remember as well to do all of this in tandem with your daily set routine, which should be something like the following:

1. **Put down on a sheet of paper the current price of the major currencies** (EURUSD, USDCHF, USDJPY and GBPUSD), plus the AUDUSD, NZD/USD and USDCAD. From these, one can start to glean the pervasive risk sentiment in the market. A rising EUR generally means that investor appetite for risk has moved up the risk curve – that is, they are willing to take more risk – which should be cross-checked with other higher-risk currencies, such as the AUD and NZD, which, if the EUR has strengthened, should probably also have strengthened. The reverse, of course, is true. If there is a divergence in patterns then one has to find out what specific reasons are there for the AUD and NZD to weaken if the EUR is strengthening? Of course, one also has to find out why the EUR is strengthening in the first place as well.

2. **Look at overnight news and data releases** and examining the charts of each to discern trading trends, long and short term (which I would already have done previously, if I had positions on).

3. In order to discern the pervasive risk sentiment of the market, **look at the USD against other standard currencies** (GBP is good in this respect, as it is not part of the EUR-zone), as the USD is generally at the moment lower down the risk curve than the EUR.

4. **Look at the traditional safe-haven assets:** money will flow broadly into CHF, JPY and gold, although this latter haven has been corrupted recently by central bank interference (many banks produce relative risk charts, showing the current 'safe-haven' assets) when there is a sense of heightened risk in the markets and vice-versa when there is not.

5. **Read everything serious** that you can lay your hands on regarding developments overnight. I say 'serious' because reading a number of self-styled 'authoritative publications' can send one entirely up the wrong path. For reasons of legal liability, I cannot name any of these publications; suffice it to say that they are often to be found on the desks of credit ratings agencies' reception areas, which may explain why they failed to downgrade any major Western banks just prior to their complete collapse in the past few years. The chart below (although there are countless examples to choose from) might further help to illustrate my point.

EURUSD (1 Year, Daily)

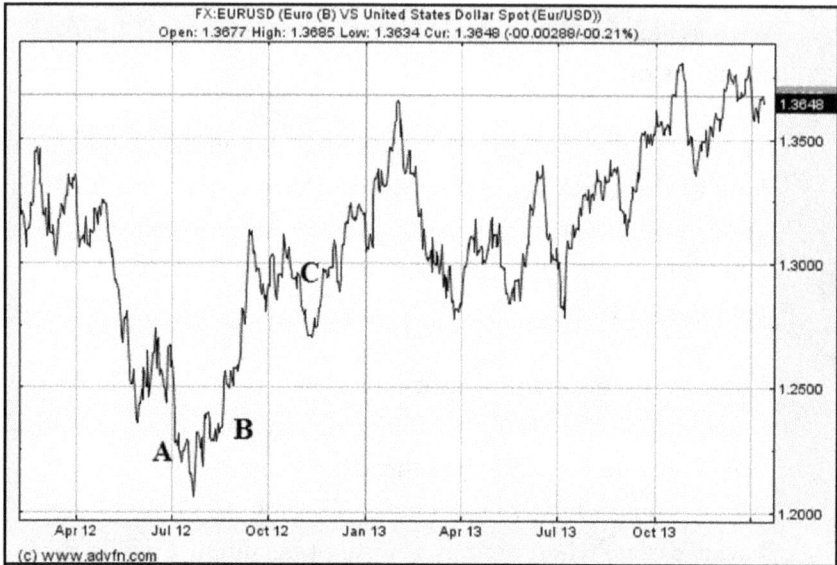

FX:EURUSD (Euro (B) VS United States Dollar Spot (Eur/USD))
Open: 1.3677 High: 1.3685 Low: 1.3634 Cur: 1.3648 (-00.00288/-00.21%)

(c) www.advfn.com

[Chart Key:
A = 'Euro chaos', well respected UK economic and political magazine
B = 'Euro nearing the end of the road', prestigious financial newspaper
C = 'Euro bears to gather pace', US financial newspaper]

6. Do the **simple technical analysis**, including plotting the day's support and resistance levels (having previously plotted the longer-term ones) and see what momentum there is behind different levels (RSI, MA Price Oscillator and so on).

7. **Check the major news and data releases scheduled for the day,** tomorrow and the remainder of the week and month, and make a note of the news/data release, the time (in GMT) that it is expected, what the data/news was on its last release and what the market consensus is for the upcoming release.

8. **Call two or three contacts in the market if you know any** – major dealers at global bank currency desks preferably – and talk to them about their thoughts on the day ahead, making notes as you go.

9. Then make a cup of tea and mull over everything that you have seen/read/heard in the past hour/couple of hours. **Then decide what you are going to do**: asset class/classes that I am going to trade, weightings of each, stop-loss and take-profit order levels and possible hedging strategies to get out of positions that turn bad.

Remember as well that **not doing anything is also an option**: if no trade stands out, with at least the correct risk/reward ratio that you have set (this should be at the very least 4:1, all factors remaining equal) then one would be best advised to do something else (read a book unconnected to the markets, go for a walk, feed the goldfish).

In summary: proper trading involves no element of gambling/risk whatsoever – it is a cold-hearted, ruthless profession (with the competition and yourself), unforgiving of taking shortcuts – and if you're in it for kicks, do something else.

If you're in it to make big money and change your life in the process, and not be one of the many who fail, then learn everything you can about the nuances of trading, keep up to speed on market-related developments around the world at all times, be self-disciplined to the point of obsession and give up believing in luck.

ABOUT THE AUTHOR

After graduating from Oxford University with BA (Hons) and MA (Hons) degrees, Simon Watkins worked for a number of years as a senior Forex trader and salesman, ultimately achieving the positions of **Director of Forex at Bank of Montreal and Head of Forex Institutional Sales for Credit Lyonnais.** He has since become a **financial journalist, being Head of Weekly Publications And Managing Editor and Chief Writer of Business Monitor International, Head of Global Fuel Oil Products for Platts, Global Managing Editor of Research for Renaissance Capital (Moscow)** and **Head of Developed Market Bond Analysis for Bond Radar.**

He has written extensively on Forex, equities, bonds and commodities for many publications, including: *The Financial Times, Euromoney, FT Capital Insights, FX-MM, CFO Insight, The Edge Middle East Finance, International Commerce Magazine, The Securities And Investment Review, Accountancy Magazine, The Emerging Markets Monitor, Asia Economic Alert, Latin America Economic Alert, Eastern Europe*

Economic Alert, Oil And Gas Middle East, European CEO, Global Finance Magazine, World Finance Magazine, The Emerging Markets Report, FTSE Global Markets, VM Group Energy Monthly, VM Group Metals Monthly, Islamic Investor Magazine, Finance Europe, Finance Emerging Europe and *CIMA Financial Management*.

In addition, he has worked as an investment consultant for major hedge funds in London, Moscow and the Middle East.

This is Simon's second book for ADVFN Books. Turn over for details of his first.

ALSO BY SIMON WATKINS

Everything You Need To Know About Making Serious Money Trading The Financial Markets

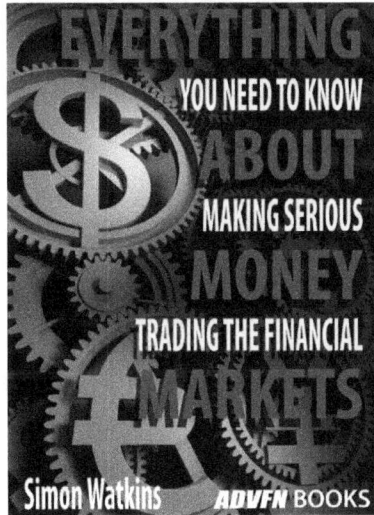

All over the world, people are trading on the financial markets. Some of them make a fortune – and many more lose their shirts. This book tells you how to be one of the winners.

It's a stark and sobering fact that around 90% of retail traders lose all of their trading money within about 90 days. That's because they have little grasp of the realities, technicalities, psychology and nature of the financial markets. In short, they don't know what they are doing.

Everything You Need To Know About Making Serious Money Trading The Financial Markets teaches you how to avoid being one of the 90%, and explains how to stack the odds firmly in your favour so you can become one of the 10% that make life-changing money trading. It's a trading bible that covers all aspects of the subject, from the psychology of trading and the mindset you need to succeed, through the fundamental principles that should guide your trades, to the trading methodologies that will help you succeed.

Fully illustrated with detailed charts, the book shows how you can use technical analysis to make your decisions, how to manage your risk and how to take out hedge positions to offset possible losses.

MORE BOOKS FROM ADVFN

101 CHARTS FOR
TRADING SUCCESS

by Zak Mir

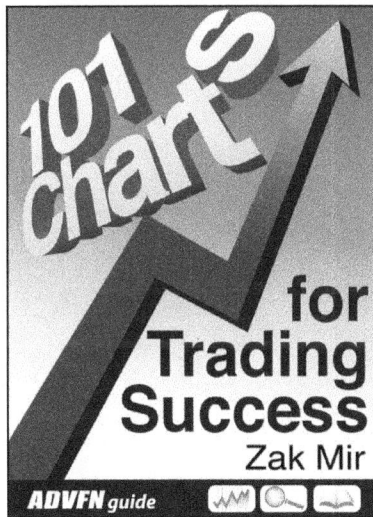

Using insider knowledge to reveal the tricks of the trade, Zak Mir's *101 Charts for Trading Success* explains the most complex set ups in the stock market.

Providing a clear way of predicting price action, charting is a way of making money by delivering high probability percentage trades, whilst removing the need to trawl through company accounts and financial ratios.

Illustrated with easy to understand charts this is the accessible, essential guide on how to read, understand and use charts, to buy and sell stocks. *101 Charts* is a must for all future investment millionaires.

THE GAME IN WALL STREET

by Hoyle and Clem Chambers

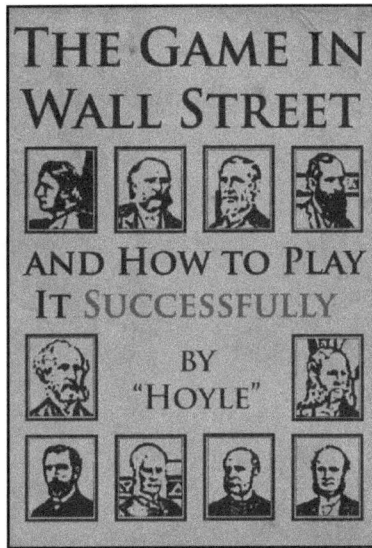

As the new century dawned, Wall Street was a game and the stock market was fixed. Ordinary investors were fleeced by big institutions that manipulated the markets to their own advantage and they had no comeback.

The Game in Wall Street shows the ways that the titans of rampant capitalism operated to make money from any source they could control. Their accumulated funds gave the titans enormous power over the market and allowed them to ensure they won the game.

Traders joining the game without knowing the rules are on a road to ruin. It's like gambling without knowing the rules and with no idea of the odds.

The Game in Wall Street sets out in detail exactly how this market manipulation works and shows how to ride the price movements and make a profit.

And guess what? The rules of the game haven't changed since the book was first published in 1898. You can apply the same strategies in your own investing and avoid losing your shirt by gambling against the professionals.

Illustrated with the very first stock charts ever published, the book contains a new preface and a conclusion by stock market guru Clem Chambers which put the text in the context of how Wall Street operates today.

THE DEATH OF WEALTH

by Clem Chambers

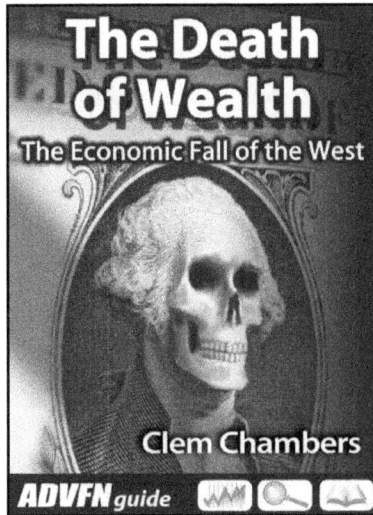

Question: what is the next economic game changer?
Answer: The Death of Wealth.

Market guru Clem Chambers dissects the global economy and the
state of the financial markets and lays out the evidence for the death
of wealth.

The Death of Wealth flags up the milestones on the route towards
impending financial disaster. From the first tentative signs of
recovery in the UK and US stock markets at the start of 2012, to the
temporary drawing back from the edge of the Fiscal Cliff at the end,
the book chronicles the trials and tribulations of the markets
throughout the year.

Collecting together articles and essays throughout the last twelve
months along with extensive new analysis for 2013, *The Death of*

Wealth allows us to look at these tumultuous events collectively and draw a strong conclusion about what the future holds.

2012 started with the US economy showing signs of recovery, and European financial markets recovering some of the ground lost during the euro crisis. It ended with Obama's re-election and the deal that delayed the plunge off the fiscal cliff by a few months.

In between, the eurozone crisis continued, but none of the affected countries actually left the eurozone; quantitative easing tried to turn things around with the consequences of these "unorthodox" actions yet unknown; and the equity markets after the mid-year correction became strongly bullish.

The Death of Wealth takes you through the events of 2012 month by month, with charts showing the movements of the FTSE 100, the NASDAQ COMPX and the SSE COMPX throughout the year.

With an introduction by renowned market commentator and stock tipster Tom Winnifrith and a summary by trading technical analyst Zak Mir, this collection chronicles the rocky road trip the financial systems of the world have been on and predicts the ultimate destination: the death of wealth as we know it.

For more information go to the ADVFN Books website at www.advfnbooks.com.

ADVFN BOOKS

www.ingramcontent.com/pod-product-compliance
Lightning Source LLC
Chambersburg PA
CBHW060021210326
41520CB00009B/956